Naked

and

You

Clothed

Me

a spiritual retrospective
from the yellow satchel!

**

Ann Bowes

Published by Book Castle Publishing

ISBN 978-1-906632-15-1

Printed in Great Britain

Dedicated to Paul - the warp to the weft in the fabric of my life

Special thanks to
Michael Matthews and Maureen East for their generous technical expertise in helping to prepare this book for publication: Hillsprint for the cover
layout and design

Cover pictures:
   Author at Thormanby Harvest Festival, with her
      home-grown pumpkin © Brian Barber
   Author outside Hockliffe House with her beloved 2CV

Unless otherwise indicated, Bible quotations are taken from the New International Version

Then the King will say to those on His right hand, 'Come, you blessed of my Father; inherit the kingdom prepared for you from the foundation of the world: for I was hungry and you gave Me food; I was thirsty and you gave Me drink; I was a stranger and you took Me in; I was naked and you clothed Me; I was sick and you visited Me; I was in prison and you came to Me.'
                                    Matthew 25: 34-36 (Authorised Version)

Contents

Shakespeare: As You Like It

The Seven Ages of Man

All the world's a stage, and all the men and women merely players. They have their exits and their entrances, and one man in his time plays many parts, his acts being seven ages.

At first the infant, mewling and puking in the nurse's arms.

And then the whining schoolboy with his satchel and shining morning face, creeping like snail unwillingly to school.

And then the lover, sighing like furnace, with a woeful ballad made to his mistress' eyebrow.

Then a soldier, full of strange oaths, and bearded like the pard, jealous in honour, sudden, and quick in quarrel...

And then the justice, in fair round belly... full of wise saws and modern instances; and so he plays his part.

The sixth age shifts into the lean and slipper'd pantaloon, with spectacles on nose and pouch on side, his youthful hose well sav'd a world too wide for his shrunk shank...

Last scene of all, that ends this strange, eventful history, is second childishness and mere oblivion, sans teeth, sans eyes, sans taste, sans everything.

Naked and you clothed me

The Seven Ages of Woman

At first the infant, shawl wrapped, mewling and puking in the mother's arms.

And then the tentative schoolgirl, uniformed with satchel and shining morning face, creeping like snail unwillingly to school and intrepidly on through adolescence.

And then the elegant lover, sighing like furnace, and with gentle mother's woven ballad.

And then the feminist woman (what no bra?), full of strange and new experiences; lifestyle challenged, sudden and quick in energy, spontaneous in decision for better or worse!

And then, to sing the new song of wisdom and ancient instances, and so she plays her costumed part.

The sixth stage shifts into yet a new melody to be composed, with body now managing sans oestrogen, with spectacles on nose; the youthful hose now somewhat too snug a fit.

Last scene of all that ends this strange, eventful history... sans everything? Not yet. Now with another satchel, this time a yellow one!.

Author's Notes

Most of this book has been written 'today' but, with their different contemporary perspectives, some of these pieces were written a number of years ago. They have been lightly edited to suit their appearance in this narrative, but their viewpoint has not been amended through the benefit of hindsight. They can be identified by their earlier dating next to the heading.

Spiritual Reflection

Woven into the book are spiritual reflections which I have shared with others in my ministry over the decades. 'Reflection' by its very nature implies that, when we dare to look thoughtfully and with fresh eyes into a mirror, we may see something more of who we are which can enrich our understanding and our growth. I offer them here because it is actually where the impetus and insight for this clothing exploration began.

Garments matter in the ancient stories of other times, cultures and in the Bible, just as they do today. Miracles really happened around some of them in Biblical accounts! What these people clothed their nakedness with was significant.

It is no wisdom to dismiss discerning consideration of clothing as 'frivolous vanity'. It matters what we do within them or without them! We have a responsibility to those garments which serve us well, to allow them to become part of our reality and joy, coexisting in their relationship with our nakedness, body, mind and spirit. They proclaim to others who we are and to be deprived of that gracious freedom of choice is painful at a deep level. I am reminded of a film in the Imperial War Museum which includes 'clothing' as part of the healing process for those liberated from WW2 concentration camps. In this film, how holocaust survivors responded to the impact of this new clothing arriving into camps is demonstrated by how people came to life - apathy and exhaustion reduced - once they could sort through the piles of garments and choose what they would wear.

Clothes and what we do in them matter. I recall a gloriously disrespectful and scary comment one day in a Yorkshire village,

"'Ow can yer trust a vicar 'oo walks down Main Street in 'is dog collar, eatin' a pastie?"

We have been warned!

Preface

Dress has never been a straightforward business: so much subterranean interest and complex feeling attaches to it. As a topic, it is popular because it is dangerous – it has a flowery head but deep roots in the passions. On the subject of dress almost no-one, for one or another reason, feels truly indifferent: if their own clothes do not concern them, somebody else's do.
Elizabeth Bowen

I recognise this! I had a friend in my late twenties who spoke of my new maxi- coat, "Very Ann Bowes, but I wouldn't be seen dead in it!"

Reaching the traditional three score years and ten, I look back on seven decades of enjoying, celebrating and sometimes agonising around my clothing choices. I have learned that style is little to do with fashion. I now consider that the promptings of who we are inside define what we wear over our nakedness and that this statement can in turn define us to others.

This is not an academic study, a fashion manual or a book about expensive designer clothing, but a gathering of life stories hung on clothes. So it is not a fully-fledged autobiography, but a loose collection of sketches and vignettes. They follow several incarnations of my chaotic and varied professional and family life, with occasional stories of clothes significant to others, all augmented by literary quotes and spiritual reflections.

I invite you to open the door, enter the wardrobe, decade after decade, and enjoy!

© Rebecca Honeywell

Timeline

Hockliffe House

Prologue

Retiring by Nature

So, out I go!

I retired from ministry in my sixties to a village not far away but in another Diocese (the unwritten rule). We were there for three years and, in retrospect, this became a time of retreat and recovery. In the field at the bottom of the garden were cows, with calves feeding from their mothers, and there was even a bull. I enjoyed watching the 'courting rites' of this bull which was not all 'wham bam thank you ma'am', which you might imagine when you think of a bull in a china shop. No, he would quietly sidle up alongside one of them and gently and slowly run his head along the length of her flank over and over again. Is it because they were nursing mothers that he was so gentle and undemanding? I like to think so.

In those times The Barchester Chronicles was excellent reading material. Of course, I was drawn to them not only because I could see that little had changed in terms of the established church over two centuries; yet also because of their literary style of irony and humour I began to recover!

Trollope in Barchester Towers writes of the dress of the bishop's wife in a significant nomenclature!

Mrs Proudie had no idea of being less thought of than the chaplain. She was beginning to be stately, stiff and offended when unfortunately the caster of the sofa caught itself in the lace train and carried away there is no saying how much of her garniture. Gathers were heard to go, plaits to fly open, flounces were seen to fall, and breadths to expose themselves; a long ruin of rent lace disfigured the carpet.

And from insights in that brilliant work into the portrayal of characterisation via clothing has come this exploration for me around what we wear to clothe our nakedness, in all its fascination, contradiction and irony, encrypted in our choices.

I now sometimes serve as a lay preacher in a busy, outward-looking United Reformed Church in a market town, and have experienced great joy in returning to my nonconformist roots. Also, I still work as a freelance funeral celebrant.

On Paul's retirement we moved to a larger, gloriously remote farm cottage nearby as tenants, with a flexible rent which is part paid by undertaking tasks for the landlord. Thus, ironing shirts, gardening, occasionally looking after dogs, planting trees, sawing logs, beating for shoots and generally making ourselves invisible! We are well supplied with partridge and pheasant in season and Paul can now 'sort them out'!

The description of 'cottage' underplays its size. It even has two spare bedrooms in what I call an East Wing. So now we have a family gathering place yet again...and they do. Up they come from the south. The next generation comprises six grandchildren (soon seven, maybe more anon!), and once one lot is coming that seems to attract the rest! The Aga does struggle when they are all here as it is of very ancient lineage, but we manage. And, of course, the dwelling needs to be big enough to house all the BOOKS!

January 2018

So, where did my 'call' begin? "I have called you by name – you are mine..."

Isaiah 43: 1

Principal Dramatis Personae

Ann: author (1947)

Paul: husband (1947)

Betty: mother (1924-2015)

Bert: father (1923)

Jane: sister (1949)

Sue: sister (1951)

Richard: brother (1966)

Emma: daughter (1970) - husband Lorenzo

Jeremy: son (1972) - wife Elaine, sons Oliver and Elliot

Hannah: daughter (1976) - husband Mark, sons Joshua and Harry

Tim: son (1979) - wife Ruth

William: son (1980) - wife Louise, daughter Lottie, son Bertie

Chapter 1

At first the infant, shawl wrapped, mewling and puking in the mother's arms.

Brand New

1947 – 1957

In which I am born in a Birmingham suburb...eldest of three sisters...Brownies and cathedrals...first church experience..."Ann loves going to Sunday School."

1

The First Age

Naked and you clothed me
i)   Sartorial Elegance in Sparkhill
ii)   Laundry, 39,000 shirts
iii)   Re-membering
iv)   Handmade Clothes
v)   Bert the Beret
vi)   Then Mum started Brownies
vii)   Plaits, Ringlets and Itchy Socks go to Shard End Baptist
viii)   Three Sisters
ix)   Fish and Chip Vests
x)   Harry of Style and Wisdom Wears the Feather
xi)   Oliver's Choir Robes

Naked and you called me
xii)   Samuel's new Coat
        Can loss in our life come to be seen less as an affliction of darkness than of angels of light, calling us to all that can yet be discovered?
xiii)   It's Not Fair. Joseph's Coat of Many Colours
xiv)   Battle Garments. Do we keep our faces in a jar by the door?

Naked and you clothed me

Sartorial Elegance in Sparkhill
Written in 2013-2014

You created my inmost being; you knit me together in my mother's womb. My frame was not hidden from you when I was woven together... Psalm 139:13,15

Naked, and wrapped only in slipperiness, I slithered and tumbled out of my mother, landing in the waiting and welcoming hands of the midwife. I have arrived.

I glimpsed my first day in the midst of a memorably rare Brummie heat-wave in 1947 at my grandparents' home in Sparkhill, Birmingham, (it says so on my birth certificate). My parents, two younger sisters and I lived with them until just before the Coronation in 1953. My 1950s housewife Mum was certainly very busy, while Dad was always at work in wake-time hours, being a bread rounds-man from dawn to dusk. The only thing I remember of him really from those days was my relishing picking over his cold kipper bones before Mum washed up the plate; and Dad being at home on Sundays when I would never eat my dinner, but enough said about the psychological aspect of *that* attention–seeking scenario!

Grandma was a pioneering milk lady with a horse and cart, working for the Co-op, (260229 was our divvi number). She had to be the one to go out to work, as my Grandad was twenty years older and had retired early from the Post Office with heart problems. So he was the adult who would 'be about' and 'have time'. I have a few fleeting memories of him in those early days, but one especially; I remember it as a regular event, but in hindsight it may only have happened once, and must have been hugely significant.

He was a striking man and the background to why he was much older than Grandma, who was a barmaid when they met, is, because of 'those days', shrouded in mystery, and we do not dare go there with my mother, even now. But Grandad was always described as 'a toff'. I recall setting off with him one sunny morning. He held my hand. He had thick, snowy white hair, and on this occasion was wearing a dark suit, sporting a large red carnation in his button-hole, and tapping along with what I now know was an ebony cane topped by an elaborately engraved silver knob. (Maybe that is the moment when I began to adore unsuitable clothing.) I shall never forget how, at this tender age, I was overwhelmed with the wonder of it.

It got better. We turned right along the main road until we came to Bar-clays Bank (or the betting shop... not sure which, they were next door to each other), where we were joined on a bench outside by other of his old gentlemen friends, and he bought me an ice cream cornet. This was a very rare treat in-deed for those days. Perhaps from a bike and cart 'Stop me and buy one'! It could be that was where began what appears to have been a feature of my min-istry - an empathy with elderly gentlemen, particularly with snowy white hair. But

3

others come nowhere near to the elegance of my Grandad, observed and noted that morning when I was about three years old and never forgotten since.

Peacocks and peahens come to mind. If I remember my Grandma's clothing from those days at all, it will be seeing her in a brown coat/overall, coming in from work. (I think they were called cow-gowns. So maybe that is why I fell in love aged twelve during Guide Camp with the cow milking man in Malvern Wells, who wore one likewise.) My humble, unconditionally loving, generous Grandma. She bought us the comics our parents wouldn't buy for us - School Friend, Bunty, Jackie. I heard grown-ups say of her, 'We always thought she might have some 'gypsy' in her'. Maybe that's where the 'other sight' gene comes from in our female family line.

Genes? Maybe my passion for, and involvement with, much funeral work throughout my mature years derives from Grandad's heritage, along with the shared over the top clothes eccentricity. His family, it is believed, were reputable funeral directors and monumental masons in Yardley, Birmingham during the nineteenth century. Well, they all dress up still, don't they... top hats and the like? Oh yes, and of course, the cane. H'm! maybe that is its provenance?

Because here is the sequel. The day after I wrote the above, the cane was 're-discovered' and given to me as custodian for posterity, via my younger sister. Apparently, Paul had been carrying it around in his car for weeks, waiting to decide what to do with it for me in terms of restoration! That he should choose this moment to hand it over unrepaired, just as I am writing about it, is classic serendipity. I cannot tell you the astonishment, joy and gratitude I have experienced on being re-united with it. It also helps me to feel that my writing is alive and evolving with a life of its own. I am not a person who overvalues material possessions (well except maybe my clothes), but this is so precious now. The silver top is broken and battered and needs replacement, but is still hall marked and beautifully engraved. From its length, Grandad must have been a shortish man, although I remember him as being quite tall, but then he would have seemed so, next to three- year-old me, wouldn't he?

As I handled that cane over the next few days after having seen it only in my mind's eye for over 60 years, it became obvious that it was more than a walking stick. Was it something to do with another part of the world; another culture? Religious? A ceremonial cane, because it was marked at the top with what looked like symbolic engravings? At the end of yesterday, winging into my brain came an answer, Of course, black and silver! It is a funeral cane! Yes; my dear mother remembered that Nibbs, an ancestor, was a funeral director and monumental mason! After investigation it is suggested that this cane could even be late 18th Century.

One year has passed, and now I have the beautiful cane, stunningly and exquisitely restored, with a new engraved top, in the Jewellery Quarter in Birmingham, its probable city of provenance, and yet the shaft of the cane still has an African 'sensing' about it.

The week it arrived, my eleven-year-old grandson, Joshua, and I took it with us to a silent, outdoor, night-time commemoration of those who died in the First World War on its 100th Anniversary, 4th August 2014. We thought it appropriate to take the cane as Grandad had fought in that war. (My paternal Grandad had undertaken his war service by training and breaking in mules and horses for the battlefield.) Joshua solemnly walked with the cane, the new silver knob cradled in his palm. He remarked, 'Grandma. When I do this I can sort of feel all the stories this stick has told and been through in its lifetime.'

As for Grandad's buttonhole flower, I have also just read that one of the earliest precedents was set by Louis XV1, to whom Parmentier had given a potato flower in the hope of making the unloved root vegetable fashionable. Soon a flower became the essential accessory of elegance for all men, even the most strict. And as for Grandad's elegant suit, my mother tells me it spent most weekends in those days in the pawn shop!

**

We move on a little further to more of the history (or her story) into which I was born. We humbly explore the recurring significance of laundry...

******

Laundry. 39,000 Shirts.

In our current semi-retirement we live as tenants on a remote farm in North Yorkshire. There is an understanding that I iron the landlord's and his sons' shirts every week. This arrangement leads me to reflect that probably over my fifty years of shirt ironing tasks for a husband, five children, and now a landlord and his family, I reckon on having made smooth, flat and immaculate on average about fifteen a week, during that time reaching the grand total of some

5

39,000. I recognize that I am 'ironically' in the very shoes of both my grand-mothers. That gives me a joyful chuckle.

Dashing away with a smoothing iron!

Both my grandmothers took in washing to help the money go round – one who was already the main bread-winner anyway via her milk round with horse and cart, and the other with a clever but lazy husband, a portion of whose meagre earnings found their way to the Off Licence, or as it was called then, the outdoor, as opposed to the 'indoor' when you went into the pub for a tankard!

My maternal grandmother talked of her laundry processing as soaking, boiling, blue bag, washing, starching, scrubbing, mangling, drying, ironing (heating irons on the fire), crimping, airing and folding. However, yesterday I heard some lovely laundry snippets from my Dad, who was the collector and delivery boy for the washing his mother did for others. This could involve him in walking an eight to ten-mile trip around Birmingham suburbs. His delivery vehicles were sometimes a wheelbarrow and sometimes his younger brother's pram, when my Dad would scoot at great speed along the pavements, one foot on one of the mudguards. I am not sure whether the youngster was in the pram with the washing or not. It could explain a lot!

Washed and processed laundry would do the return journey in brown paper carriers. His main, rather wicked memory is of his teacher's washing being done by his mother; he was six at the time and still remembers her long 'coms' blowing like balloons on his home washing line, and then he would eventually sit in her class and remember!

6

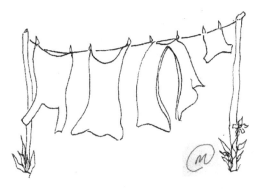

Tentatively and precariously pegged onto my lifeline

      I read a novel recently which had a huge impact on me and spoke of black servants of the Sixties in white households in America. This powerful and deeply shocking account of life as experienced when racial discrimination cruelly 'rules' is called The Help. Written in the first person, as if by the black servant, Kathryn Stockett's work has also been made into a film. Here is a laundry extract; the dress referred to belongs to a skinny, mean and spiteful person:

She already got the blue dress on I ironed this morning, the one with sixty-five pleats on the waist, so tiny I got to squint through my glasses to iron. I don't hate much in life but me and that dress are not on good terms.

**

Remember... In its real sense it means to re-member, i.e. put together the 'members' or parts of the past into a present whole. I wrote the following reflection one Remembrance Sunday morning whilst I was caring for my mother in my parents' retirement bungalow...

******

Re-membering
Written in 2012

      It is November. I am writing this around 11.00am on Remembrance Day whilst multitasking as usual, including cooking the Sunday lunch for my parents in their home. Classic FM has been sensitive and moving in its choice of music - Nimrod and the Benedictus from Carl Jenkins' Mass for the Common Man, and of course the Last Post with two minutes' silence. I recalled to myself how important this remembering is in its true sense of re-membering; putting the memory together again, with insight.

This cosy bungalow in the Shropshire countryside is internally almost identical to the home where we grew up (on a newly constructed council estate built for ex-servicemen and their families) in Birmingham nearly 70 years ago. The furniture

7

is the same and placed in the same way. It's still the only place I know where, when you need to write something down in a hurry, the fountain pens or biros are never empty and the pencils are always sharpened into fine, yet stout leads, which don't snap off and fall out when you apply them to the page!

My Dad at nearly 90 has set off to the village memorial for the service. He looked and walked as if he were about twenty years younger, I'd say; very upright and smart in navy blazer, beret and medals. He went to re-member. He was a Normandy veteran on Landing Craft, having to urge young soldiers onto Sword Beach. He re-members that in those days he was the humblest of Able Seamen, but now, due to his fitness, longevity and sharpness of mind, he is increasingly saluted and honoured as a hero. He was asked recently by a young man how he could have been involved in that task against all his gentle and gracious human instincts; he replied that he was of a generation brought up to do as they were told without questioning...total obedience.

The pie in the oven, I went in to sit quietly alongside my mother in her early stages of dementia. She was sleeping on the saggy old sofa, frail and dozing and completely dependent on my father now, even in the choice of clothes she would wear each day. This was so sad in the light of her earlier passion and skills for dress-making of the highest quality and stylish outfits. I remembered her too and the powerhouse she had been, bringing up a large family as a full-time housewife. Highly intelligent, gifted, stunning then in her hand-crafted outfits. The bringing up of us all was down to her. She managed all the money (very little), made all our clothes, encouraged us all in our education and sorted out the family hassles. I don't think my father ever faced a real conflict after Normandy, and it is my Mum who has had to face and endure all the upheavals, battles and conflicts of family life ever since. I feel in some ways Dad wears the medals and Mum bears the battle scars of family life. For many women of that generation and beyond, this may well be true and I am reminded of these words in Women who run with the Wolves by Clarissa Pinkola Estees, who speaks of the honour as well as the pain of those scars. She urges:

8

Count your years by scars, not years...what will our granddaughters think of our lives recorded thus? You have earned these by the hard choices of your life.

**

But she really blossomed and flourished as a young mum, and pride in one's clothes, was certainly central to the example she set before her little daughters, or as Bel Mooney writes, 'Even if you don't have much money, always dress to impress'...

******

Handmade Clothes

I heard yesterday on Radio 3 on International Women's Day, that a composer has recently written some music for the Uncommon Woman! Our mother was one such, with very high standards in all aspects of life from dress to behaviour, for herself and actually for everyone else, it has to be said! Busy, energetic; for her, right was right and wrong was wrong. Duty and justice were paramount. She dared to face confrontation on behalf of any of us, sometimes at a cost. Thus, homemaking, bringing up her children and caring for them and her husband, was central to her life; hospitable and sociable, artistically gifted and creative. She knitted, crocheted, sewed and baked to a high degree of excellence. With scraps of left over material she made patchwork bedspreads; splash, splash of vibrant colour and shape and memory and all a tribute to Mum's craftsmanship, industry and her care to recycle and 'waste-not, want-not', long before it became a LAW to recycle. These patches would remind us of the dresses, blouses and nighties we had worn and would cover our shared double bed; gingham, cotton prints all bordered and embroidered and herring-boned together on an old sheet backing.

She also had a caring for the environment before it became an issue of political awareness. We all remember her campaign against fluoride in water and toothpaste. We could not have the lovely minty squibby tubes which everyone else had, but only the flat tins of pink stuff with NO fluoride and no taste at all. Also I recall with some mystification my Mum wearing her hat all day on Sundays both inside and outside the house, including for meals! Dinners were a bit terrifying in retrospect...stuffed hearts, tripe and onions, soused herrings. But then Sundays were a busy time in our family; three church services throughout the day. I recall one Sunday in particular Mum looking beautiful in a dark green, shot silk dress and apricot hat, doing battle with a fire extinguisher outside the church building with the nozzle pointing in the wrong direction!

The happiest time of her life was when her children were small. She made all our clothes, under to over, from knitted socks and vests, cotton petti-

9

coats, even cotton knickers with lace edging, through dresses, knitted itchy jumpers, cardigans and kilts, to coats; plus any fancy dress outfits, school play costumes of the angels and shepherds nature, but once I seem to remember a frog even. The prizewinning Queen of Hearts outfit of course came complete with a tray of baked jam tarts.

She was always slender herself and thereby disparaging of any woman who was different from her trim 34.24.35 shape. 'They must be lazy or eat too much between meals!' Her enviable figure became an increasing matter of pride, eventually leading to a dramatic 'statement' in her eighties. She almost left her much loved choir when the conductor changed the uniforms for the women to blouses that did not tuck in but skimmed the waists and hips which were beginning to spread a little in middle and old age. Then trousers were added to the ensemble instead of skirts ('we're not tenors or basses') and that became the last straw.

In similar vein regarding standards of fitness she would be somewhat dismissive to observe people with their rambling boots and walking poles on the Malvern Hills as she strode onwards and upwards effortlessly in her Clarks sandals!

**

This was the lifestyle expectation into which I and my two sisters were born in the forties and fifties. But my father's defining clothing item had already been established – his hat. It was a trilby (even worn on the beach) in those early days but more latterly and even more distinctively...

******

Bert the Beret
Written in 2015

A man is more firmly bound to his hat than to his wife. He may put away the latter; without the former, life becomes a hollow mockery, for the hat makes the man. Without it he remains forever a boy.
Korean Textiles, Art and Dress. Ruth Bottomley.

Recently I called to collect my Dad's shopping order from his local village shop. 'Tell them it is for Bert the Beret,' he instructed.

I write this on holiday in Cornwall, preparing to wander off to Falmouth for the day. Dad (Bert) recalls, 'I remember coming into that amazing harbour with prisoners of war on board our ship. I was ordered to take one of them on deck to throw all his German money into the sea. He gazed disbelievingly out onto Falmouth and its beauty of landscape and seascape, and pronounced, "This not England. England flat." Had they all been told that England was defeated and that there was no landscape of beauty left at all?

10

For most of our childhood we never ever heard about Dad's war service. In Birmingham we were surrounded by its aftermath of bombed factories and houses around the gas works, with the walls blown off so you could see wallpaper hanging in strips in halls and bedrooms alongside blasted halves of staircases. I would sit on the 55 'buzz' and imagine the families who had lived there. Whatever happened to those people whose home it had been? I am still astounded that I was born only two years after the end of the war and yet it was never mentioned, except to see in the photograph album black and white photographs of my jolly, handsome dad with his shipmates in his bellbottom trousers, jaunty cap and lanyard, always smiling and looking like something out of South Pacific. This cap, he tells me, was called a Seaman's cap. When these trusty Able Seamen went to collect their weekly pay, they had to approach the pay desk and take off their hats which they presented as a receptacle for the £3. 6 shillings. I understand they also had to remove the cap if they were approaching the disciplinary table, called 'off caps'. Could this be the root of the phrase 'cap in hand', if you are approaching in sorrow or shame?

My Dad is very proud of his beret-wearing in his eighties and nineties. First because he is a Francophile and loves being in France, even though his only expertise in the language is limited to 'Le grand lit, s'il vous plait?' But as time went on, it was actually more to do with his Normandy Landing on Sword Beach in 1944. He told me recently that, even walking through Birmingham today, if his beret is worn in the correct, specific manner, he will be saluted by those with whom it generates respect and recognition. The badge being worn over the left eye, with the beret pulled down over the right ear indicates that he is a retired serviceman to those who are 'in the know'!

Normandy veteran

11

After numerous earlier commemorative trips to Normandy, during the 70th anniversary occasion he was even interviewed by BBC TV for having received the highest honour that France could award, The Légion d'Honneur. I sat with my Mum in a respite care home to watch that broadcast, surrounded by staff and other patients.

She had once or twice spoken of her war in a munitions factory, recalling sombrely that once when she was not at her shift, the whole place was bombed and blown up, taking one of her friends. She had longed to enlist as a Wren, but stayed home at her mother's request. She would have been the best!

She also spoke of when she was much younger during the war, when the bombs were dropping all around them in Birmingham. Her mother, on the way to the air raid shelter after the warning siren, sent her running back home to collect the milk money satchel which Grandma had left behind by mistake. My mother remembers being so very frightened.

(P.S. Apropos the hat of a Korean nature. More research tells me that this hat would be more like a porcelain object balanced on a top knot. If it fell off and broke, it became a severely punishable offence. The hat's purpose was as a sign of peace and if it fell off it indicated non-peaceable behaviour!)

**

It seems now that my parents had incorporated that terrible time into their lives and stoically moved on – this was a new world; one they had fought for, with some nostalgia for the sense of camaraderie and mutual support of folk in adversity. Yet now were to be new values, opportunities and strivings for themselves and the three daughters who were to arrive between 1947 and 1951, of whom I was the first! Epitomised maybe as I became the first Brownie in our circle! Because my mother ran the first Brownie pack in the area, she did now have a uniform!

******

Then Mum started Brownies
Written in 2015

I promise on my honour,
to do my best,
to do my duty to God and the Queen,
to help other people at all times
and to obey the Brownie law.

How exciting. A uniform. But first the toadstool.

The toadstool was central to the Brownie meeting. We used to dance around it, singing songs and making promises which we tried not to break! I recall our making the toadstool in the garden one summery day. My mum,

12

Brown Owl, took a car hub cap and a sort of fat metal tube about a foot high. In a large bucket we then mixed papier maché (i.e. newspaper and wallpaper paste) with which to coat them. There followed a glorious transformation of the whole when it dried, before being painted bright yellow with large red spots. This served the Brownie pack exceedingly effectively for many years.

I did not fare brilliantly in this organization as I was not much interested in the challenge of earning badges for sewing and the like, although I still to this day can lay and light an excellent fire. I am known in the family for my pyromaniac skills and my grandsons call me the one-match-grandma. My hospitality skills are also renowned, and I did get the book badge which has stood me in good stead ever since.

The uniform was of course very exciting. A brown, long sleeved cotton dress with large patch-pockets on the chest for pencils, notebook and a penknife with a tool for taking stones out of horses' hooves etc. (Famous Five fantasies abounded in those days.) There was a leather belt on which could be threaded a roundish, brown leather purse, and of course a bright yellow tie with pixie brass badge which needed polishing every week.

On one or two occasions we ventured forth on an intrepid Brownie pack holiday, from the city into the country, to a convent with NUNS in their habits. Black and white with sleeves rolled up to do the jobs. What an adventure.

My sister Jane recalls:

We met outside the church. A large army vehicle drew up outside with open back and a tarpaulin that could be rolled up or pulled down. We all tossed our kit bags in and clambered up to find a spot. (NO seat belts in those times.) One Brownie was already homesick, but Mum (Brown Owl) was having none of that. Off we went to Bussage, Stroud, and Gloucestershire, to stay in a convent! Days were hot and sunny, so we had a different uniform for this magical adventure. We wore a special summer short sleeved brown dress as a more informal uniform for the frolics in the Bussage convent. We were fascinated by the nuns for whom we had to organize an entertainment. My friend Janet and I practised and performed a clapping game, standing opposite each other and getting the timing right. I think we chose dressing up things from a big box for this. The District Commissioner told me off for talking in the dorm, saying 'Jane, I'm surprised at you.' I was mortified. Mum and Mrs M, Tawny Owl, were very busy and happy. There was much laughter between them but almost a tragedy. Mum nearly sleepwalked out of their open upstairs window, and we think that Mrs M must have been disturbed by her and woken up in time to stop her. I remember having rhubarb for pudding and singing 'Clean yourself inside and out, twist and turn and run about'!

My other sister Sue's more rebellious recollections:

For the first Brownie pack holiday I was too young really and didn't have a dress to fit me. I was a bit of a thin small child anyway which didn't help. Some dress must eventually have been found for me. I remember walks being too long and my getting tired but receiving no sympathy from Brown Owl! I also remember not being able to sleep during the enforced resting period and I became disruptive. The Head Guider (a head teacher) came and took me away for what turned out to be a very pleasant walk around the nuns' walled garden, with her being extremely kind and tolerant of me and talking to me gently.

I also remember doing rather too much talking after lights went out one night with my friend and us getting into trouble. Over sixty years later we are still good friends and talk too much!

Happy innocent times, but I notice a rebellion against authority even at such a young age that has stayed with me!

Ann again:

I have two enduring memories of such a holiday.

First, I remember that we had to have an hour's afternoon rest after lunch on rugs in the garden or on our beds if the weather was inclement, which it rarely ever was. I have never fully recovered from this need and still require this postprandial nap if I am to function for the rest of the day. I don't remember sun creams or hats and the like. Oh dear.

My second memory is of a 'turn' in this nuns' entertainment. However I can do it justice I cannot imagine, but I shall try.

Picture the scene. Brownies are waiting quietly in a circle in huge expectation that something stupendous is about to happen. We have been told that a man with a brown face was coming especially from India to perform a magic trick for us. He would not be able to speak to us as he did not know our language. He could not bring a real snake in a basket as that would be too dangerous but he was going to perform it as an Indian rope trick instead. We saw with awe the big thick coiled rope on the floor. (I am not sure why all the grownups were somewhat suffused by a fit of the giggles which seemed rather rude actually.) Then in came slowly a tall man dressed in long white robes, with a turban on his head, and sporting a big black beard. He was weaving from side to side, playing a recorder in a haunting, seductive, wavering tune. His eyes were fixed on the coil of rope. And suddenly the end of the rope began to shiver and rise. Slowly, slowly it went, dancing to the haunting melody. It too weaved from side to side as it rose almost to the ceiling until it languished, drooping over the beam underneath the ceiling. Brownies were breathless, spellbound literally! Grownups? Collapsed in hysterics, I am sorry to say. Not sure about the nuns. So sad that Mr Brown Owl and Mr Tawny Owl were missing for that particular spectacle, although they turned up for later in the show. Those were the days!

P.S. Addition from Sue apropos Indian Rope Trick and socks.

'I remember one of the little Talbot twins suddenly shouting out. 'Oh, that Indian is Mr. Bate (Dad), I can see his socks!'

**

Brownies was part of our church life, which strangely enough began in a rather unlikely venue. It maybe set the tone for my rather eccentric Christian calling to come...

******

Plaits, Ringlets and Itchy Socks go to Shard End Baptist!
Written in 2015

Going to church began in a cinema ballroom. The beginnings of Spurgeon Baptist Church at the edge of a newly built, post war council estate in Birmingham were an inspiration to me as a child. A small pioneering group, including my parents, met together for their Christian worship in a local cinema (no films on Sundays naturally in those days) until the day came when the new church building nearby began to be built. I remember Dad eventually being a deacon in this church and sitting on the platform, but Mum doing the pastoral visiting, e.g. to a certain Mr Bruff who had a mysterious arrangement in his sitting room whereby he slept behind an orangey brown curtain and drank Bovril. I can still recall the smell of it. Every Sunday we would set off on the bus, my parents and three identically dressed little girls. Our hair would either be in plaits with big ribbons on the ends or in ringlets which would have meant that our hair had been wound very painfully indeed in tight rags all night. Hand-knitted and itchy woolly socks were worn in winter, and white ankle socks in summer, sensible shoes or sandals; lovely little fitted overcoats with velvet collars in the winter and home-made cotton dresses with knitted cardies in the summer. In fact, looking very like all the happy children illustrations in the Peter and Jane early reading books.

It was at this point, probably when I was about seven years old, that I decided I wanted to be a missionary when I grew up. I remember so well that occasion of the stone-laying ceremony for the new building adjacent to the cinema. We were moving on and out! Mr Foreman was on the old pedal organ, vigorously playing in the street outside, 'Now Thank we all our God'. In my own child-way I knew that this intrepid and courageous journey was something of which I wanted to be a part all my life. There was even a role model for me of a woman minster in the Baptist church, unlike the institutional churches. (That was to come many years later.) Sister Florence was a single lady of seemingly ancient years, proven by her straight, sticking out grey hair under her navy-blue velour pudding basin hat, along with much more serious looking clothes than my mother ever wore in her 1950s glorious heyday. I was very inspired by such elderly ladies, yet in retrospect they were probably quite young really! But even back in those days, ministry for me was something women as well as men did! Hooray!

I recall as a very small child engaging passionately with the Old Testament stories, which I used to hear both in Sunday school and at the feet of vigorous Baptist lay preachers (usually Welsh!). I believe I did have a 'call' to a vocation right from that time. I was not a particularly intelligent or wise child, but I still recall this instinctive knowledge as 'real' and it has proven over time to be thus. How do I even now begin to write about a 'call' when this concept is so resistant to language? But I shall have a go!

Special was the story of the call of the boy Samuel. This is so real, isn't it? Here is a little boy who keeps coming in to his guardian after he is supposed to have gone to bed. 'Here I am; you called me.' 'No, I didn't. Go back to bed.' We all know it, don't we? The child persistent, the grown-up tired. Three times it happened. God called, 'Samuel, Samuel.' At last the wise old man realised that it was God calling the child. Rather than ridicule him, this man listened to, believed in and responded to Samuel. Finally, he gently said to the boy, 'Go and lie down and if he calls you again say, 'Speak Lord, for your servant is listening'.'

From experience throughout the whole of my life, including my ministry, I consider this little passage to contain all that I understand of a call. It comes unexpectedly and probably while one is doing something else. It means having an ear which is prepared to listen to God, to others and to the prompting of one's own heart. It requires the courage to risk a mistake, a willingness to dare to share one's glimmerings of discernment with those whose faith we trust and respect, and the movements of persistence and response in a willingness to serve. 'Speak Lord, for your servant is listening.' The call is to 'serve', and that means handing over the controls. It means daring to be led by another, wherever that may go. But listen to what God says then to that little boy; 'See, I am about to do something in Israel that will make the ears of everyone who hears of it tingle!' It still takes my breath away!

My pioneering spirit must have begun with my parents helping to launch a church in that most unlikely setting, and I am duly proud. It has formed my life, my faith, my inspiration to minister, my love of church music and of

course I was baptised as a believer there, and I even met my husband (surviving a three-legged football match with him) and married there!
Deo Gratias!!

**

Here is a good moment to remind ourselves of the rather scary nature and dynamic of 'three sisters'...

******

Three Sisters

You will probably need to understand the psychological strength of the bond of three sisters in order fully to follow the structure and dynamics of our family. It is a known phenomenon, deep in the human psyche. If I go to an unknown family for the first visit to help them plan a funeral service and seated there are three sisters, I know I am in for a challenge. What is this strength about? There is the strength and stability of a triangle of course, the Trinity even, and we all know about the three witches' dynamic... *Hubble bubble, toil and trouble!*

From a long forgotten novel I copied the following words, which encapsulate for me this relationship in all its strength, wisdom and ambiguity.

Three sisters are a triangle of female emotion. She knew about female threesomes, being in possession of two sisters. There was always one on the outer edge, excluded from a special intimacy between the other two. But the alliances constantly shifted in order to sustain the basic group. This was where the power lay. Nothing in known human society was as powerful as this trio of women; they very often frightened even themselves.

17

Yes. True. I recognise this! So do my sisters! We have a brother, born late to my mother when I was nineteen, and he and his wife, I think, only ever see us sisters as one person. The three witches!

In our childhood Mum created all our clothes, three new dresses each, every summer. They were all of beautiful fabric, in striking designs, with maybe smocking on viyella, and the most memorable one for me was of blue gingham with two white piqué patch pockets on which were embroidered cats' faces. I can still see to this day in my mind the bright green eyes and black whiskers.

We were always dressed identically whilst being very different little people inside. I am lost in admiration now for those identical garments which were made with love by our mother. Despite financial hardship, they were not merely utilitarian in order to keep us clothed and warm. I recall interesting buttons (e.g. the pink rabbits still to be unearthed in the giant old button tin today). There would be Lucky Locket pockets, some dresses beautifully embroidered and smocked across the yoke, and we never questioned at that stage why we were all the same. The difficult moment came when I began to ask, instead of viyella, for flock nylon such as all the other girls in our street possessed. Yes, she even did that, despite all that she must have believed about discernment and taste! It was created, pale blue nylon with pink flocked flowers and a belt of pink velvet ribbon with long streamers tumbling down the skirt. It was lined with stiff silky fabric, so stuck out a little, but this was not see-through! Well, my sisters did not have one of those!

**

Now we move for a while to stories of another family generation at a similar young stage in life, introduced by an account of Fish and Chip vests…

******

Fish and Chip Vests
Written in 2014

Despite the distracting chaos of late November and December last year, when I undertook family 'missions of mercy' round Europe and beyond, three of my grandsons aged four, six and ten were delighted to receive, as their completed Christmas presents, hats and scarves, all crafted miraculously on time during that period. They were labelled, 'Knitted for Joshua with love by Grandma in Yorkshire'; 'Knitted for Oliver with love by Grandma in Morocco'; and 'Knitted with love for Elliot by Grandma in Cyprus'. Elliot's was bright red with a green fringe on the scarf, and green tassel on the beanie hat. He told his Mum later, 'I do love my hat even though it looks like a tomato and I hate tomatoes.'

18

Subsequently I also completed a scarf for Harry ('mainly green, please, Grandma'), and I almost forgot to say that an apple green one went to Emma's toy Lammy in Riparbella, Italy... Sadly, in an oversight, the cleaners in Morocco had recently put Lammy in the washing machine for a spruce-up, and his head nearly fell off with the shock. Thus, this scarf has a dual purpose, it keeps him warm and holds his head upright!

Once you are Real you can't be ugly or shabby except to people who don't understand... you become Real

Another with multicoloured fringes went to their Great Grandma's teddy, which is becoming increasingly significant to her as she becomes older and

19

more frail. It replaced her childhood ancient, shabby but much loved bear, whom my brother in his wisdom thought it a joke to burn as the guy on one of his Nov. 5th bonfires, dressed in cub scout uniform. Say no more!

This sudden frenzy of knitting of mine, after a life-time of being a disappointment to my mother in the craft department, had begun with the Fish and Chip vests. These were requested via my current URC church. 'We need knitters please asap for Fish and Chip vests. Can you help?'

These are for African premature babies who are usually wrapped in newspaper in order to keep them warm. They have to be knitted in dense bright colours, stripes and the like, because they are never washed! One of my friends, who was married to a Ghanaian, said there would be a battle for one Fish and Chip vest knitted in emerald green and bright red stripes - their football colours apparently!

My serious grandson, seven-year-old Oliver, was overwhelmed by the wider implications of this story, so on his next visit to Yorkshire he earnestly desired to learn to knit for himself. So did his mother. Oh heck, both of them known for their intransigent refusal to be deflected from a task in hand, so they spent the week on the sofa, knitting and re-knitting scarves, including one for Jeremy's dicing-with-death commuter rides to work across London by scooter, plus another for a toy squirrel belonging to Elliot. All exciting visits planned to a range of unmissable options in York were turned down in favour of frequent visits to the wool shop in Thirsk. Patterns, wool, needles, all scrutinised and considered.

P.S. Email from Emma... *Lammy is thrilled - and proud! - to be a part of your magnum opus! He was much too humble to mention that he had originally been omitted from the worthy list - he was, after all, the inspiration behind the 2013 Spring Collection!*
Love and wobbly heads from 43-year-old Lammy!

Footnote: From 'The Velveteen Rabbit'.
'Real isn't how you are made,' said the skin horse to the Velveteen Rabbit at the nursery fender. 'It's a thing that happens to you. When a child loves you for a long, long time, not just to play with, but really loves you, then you become Real. Generally, by the time you are Real, most of your hair has been loved off, and your eyes drop out and you get loose in the joints and very shabby. But these things don't matter at all, because once you are Real you can't be ugly or shabby except to people who don't understand.'

**

And in their own very different religious contexts, two of my grandchildren share significant clothing responses...

******

20

Harry of Style and Wisdom Wears the Feather
Written in 2016

One month for three weeks running, I found myself having to preach from the lectionary on similar readings where Jesus' teaching was firmly, radically and somewhat subversively encouraging all those who believe themselves to be wise to become again as little children. What on earth (or in Heaven) did he mean? This would have been totally shocking in a culture where children were considered as lowly in the scheme of all things as slaves and beggars; in fact they were not regarded as having any status whatsoever.

As week followed week, I was beginning to run out of insightful inspiration. Obviously, I should run this dilemma by a junior oracle himself, so went to a small grandson. I asked Harry (6), 'Why does Jesus say that children are wiser than grown-ups?' He was reflective for a moment, and then came his considered response:

'Little children are wiser than grown-ups because grown-ups' heads are stuffed full of memories and work and things needing to do. Children don't have all that clutter, so they have space in their brains to believe and understand about God and Jesus and angels and things.'

He has long been interested in angels and I found in my 'treasures-for-a-useful-occasion box' a beautiful fluffy long white feather on a sort of sparkly silver looped thread, and sent it to him as a 'thank you'. Apparently, he wore it for ages at home, looped over one ear, though Harry knew instinctively that to wear it to school might be taking things a bit too far. Did it make him feel like an angel? Not for me to speculate.

I am moved to tears when I remember that Hannah, his Mum, allowed him freely to add this feather without comment to his various outfits. She was instinctively wise. The psychologist, Flugel, writes that children are less interested in integrated outfits, but prefer to be passionate about one particular item of the outfit they are wearing. He continues that it is important for parents to allow that freedom of choice, as it sets up and allows the foundation for an appropriate expression of the inner self later on.

Recent insight...Harry is in exalted company obviously. It tells me on the Twining's Lady Grey Teabag box that their esteemed lady, renowned for her beauty and elegance, frequently wore a peacock feather in her hair at social gatherings. (I wonder why she chose a male peacock feather? It must be because they are the colourful ones of the species. H'm!)

At the age of eight, he was feeling deprived in not having godparents like his Catholic cousins, and asked to be baptised. This he studied for and undertook in absolute integrity at the Easter liturgy in his little village church. He stood solemnly isolated on the plinth around the font, and made his vows to a full church, in a style appropriate to the occasion which for us all was truly unique.

**

And Oliver, his cousin?...

****

Oliver's Choir Robes
Written 2016

The following extraordinary exposition happened around the chaotic breakfast table in Yorkshire, whilst munching the toast and muesli! Ten-year-old chorister Oliver explains:

Whatever we have been doing up till then, it feels strange that as soon as we walk into the vestry we know that from then on we have to be very much more professional and mature. That is because it is so important that there is a good performance for the mass.

No matter how many times you have done it, you always feel a sense of adventure as you prepare for it because it is never the same.

There are two garments to wear, a cassock and a cotta. I would describe the cassock as being like a very long purple dress and a cotta is white with a red cross on it. That is like a short smock which reaches the waist. The cross is a sign that we who wear it are fully fledged Choristers of Westminster Cathedral. When you are only wearing a cassock, it means we are just preparing for the Mass; when you are wearing the cotta as well, it means we are all done and ready!

When it begins, you have to concentrate, stay in time and watch and listen. (His younger brother Elliot interrupts at this point and tells me that Oliver will never look at anyone else while he is in the choir, so he knows he cannot smile at him or try to distract him. Elliot too is now a chorister there.)

I almost always sing in Latin, although as yet I do not understand much about what the words mean. But I have to focus very closely to get the pronunciation right.

To be there in the choir and singing the Mass with adult singers, and to wear those robes makes me feel special because only thirty boys at the most at any one time ever wear them. It feels unique, especially after you have put them on. I enjoy wearing them. Even when the boys are not singing and it is just the men, I like to follow their music in the Graduale Romanum, the book of Gregorian chants. We only sing the Introit, Alleluia, Kyrie, Agnus Dei, Sanctus and Credo. I especially love singing big pieces like the Monteverdi Vespers. That is be-

cause they are looming, scary and exciting. It is nice to see the speciality of a composer.

The most interesting things about being a chorister may be when we can go on tours and do concerts. When you take the robes off, you go back into the world and you feel a sense of achievement. It feels as if you have sung as part of a long line of Masses in history and of many more which are to come. I will sing many more before another boy will have to replace me.

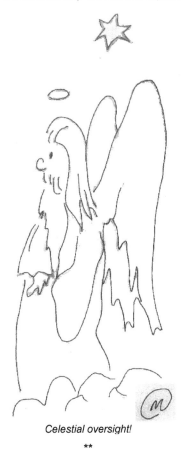

Celestial oversight!

**

Now we hear again of another little boy who served God in a temple rather than a cathedral...

******

23

Naked and you called me

Samuel's New Coat
1 Sam 2: 19

At the end of my Anglican ministry, one of my most dynamic parishioners told me that she had never forgotten one of my Mothering Sunday sermons about the boy Samuel, based on a passage from Margaret Silf's book, Sacred Spaces. It encourages, through the metaphor of a little boy's coat, a reflection on boundaries and loss in our own lives being less afflictions of darkness than angels of light calling us forward to all that is yet waiting to be discovered.

In a church service of worship on Mothering Sunday, we offer a time to remember our 'Mother church' but it has come to be a secular occasion too, where we are all encouraged, whatever our age, to give thanks for our mothers. At the conclusion of this occasion we are all invited to collect a small posy of flowers to give to our mother, or if we no longer have a mother alive or nearby we receive flowers by which to remember her. Here is something beautiful and fragrant which reminds us of the beauty of God's creation of which we are all a part. And it reminds those of us who love the mother church that we are thankful for the opportunity to come to worship and praise and thank the God who gave us life.

As a mother of five children, I certainly know the joy, but also sometimes the costly and unconditional love involved in caring for and bringing up children. Also, the cost of recognising when they have to be encouraged out of the nest! Playgroup, school, university, leaving home, marriage. Help! They may or may not be scared to fly and we may or may not be equally scared of having to let them go! But to spread their wings, and move into greater freedom, opens out life more fully for them. We may have to let go of those whom we have treasured, in order that they may grow; thus, in order that we also may have the opportunity to grow.

I sometimes think God deals with us like a mother too. Things happen in our lives. We find ourselves having to let go; of things, our health, work or people who have been precious to us. And sometimes it is difficult to understand why this has had to be so. So, I invite you to enter a beautiful Bible story about a mother and a little boy to see if we can glean insight from that today.

Margaret Silf sheds a beacon of light on the story of the little boy Samuel and his mother Hannah:

Hannah would visit Samuel in the temple every year, and each year she would take with her a little coat she had made for him. Each year it would be a bigger coat than the year before. The story moves me deeply. Amid all the paraphernalia of the Temple sacrifices and the big talk about the people's covenant with their Lord, here is a mother who knows, as only a mother can, that her little boy is growing all the time, and will need a bigger coat each year.

24

The story goes on to the next year's growing…

We too grow out of our coats. We grow out of this year's certainties and fixed positions as surely as fills up this year's diary. We can perhaps imagine little Samuel protesting each year as his mother took off the coat he had outgrown and gave him the new one in its place. For those few minutes he must have shivered and felt very exposed. But Hannah knew that if he didn't put on the bigger coat, by the end of the following year he wouldn't be able to move freely because last year's coat would be far too small for him.

When I fall into new chasms of doubt, or face new depths of loss, I try to remember Samuel. When my Mother-God strips off the outgrown garment, I try to trust she is doing so to give me space for my next year's growing. Thus doubt becomes a sacred boundary, rather than a fearful abyss; and doubt, though grievous, leads to a new gateway of being.

Can you recognise a boundary time in your own life, when you have had to risk a move from what feels safe and certain in order to be free to grow? Like a loving and caring mother, God is always there for us in our cold times, our times of loss. Our times of wondering what this is all about? She may not be able to take you back to where you were. She may offer you a coat which is just a bit too big and you might think you will never grow into it. Can you be open to trusting in that hope; that promise?

Called to Brafferton house for duty ministry in 2003; arriving on the threshold during interview…

I offer these words from Isaiah for encouragement. Hear them for yourself and for all whom you love and have loved. *'God says, (to you, to me) I have called you by name. You are mine. You are precious and honoured in my sight and I love you.'*

**

We have read of the little boy Samuel's coat and here is an account of the coat of another young boy. Samuel was his mother's only child; this next little boy was the youngest of eleven sons. Joseph's brothers were jealous of him, believing him to be their father's favourite and this special coat just about confirmed all their resentment...It's not fair! Do we recognize that?...

******

It's Not Fair. Joseph's Coat of Many Colours
Genesis 37: 3-36

It all began with a dream.

Imagine for a moment that you are one of Joseph's half-brothers. There are ten of you, strong tough men. But Joseph, the child of another of Jacob's wives, is the favourite son of your father, Jacob. How does this favouritism feel to you as one of the older sons? Not only is the youngest brother the favourite, the chosen one, the most loved, the most blessed; but their father then goes and honours that chosen-ness and special blessing by making him a richly ornamented coat in all the colours of creation. Now everyone knows!

In addition to all this chosen-ness and blessing, Joseph is also blessed in other ways; he has dreams which he can interpret with wisdom and discernment. And now here comes an outrageous dream to make this already volatile family situation even more unbearable.

Joseph had a dream, and when he told it to his brothers they hated him all the more. He said to them, 'Listen to this dream I had: we were binding sheaves of corn out in the field when suddenly my sheaf rose and stood upright, while your sheaves gathered round mine and bowed down to it.' Genesis 37: 5-7

The final straw indeed!

So they plotted together to kill their dreaming brother. At the last minute they spared him; stripped him of his beautiful coat; threw him into a cistern which mercifully contained no water; changed their minds again; hauled him out, and sold him as a slave to some passing Midianite traders. After which, they soaked Joseph's special coat in animal blood and returned to their father saying that his precious, chosen, blessed and favourite son had been torn to pieces by a ferocious animal. End of Joseph for those envious brothers; gone out of their lives forever. Chosen, blessed maybe, but now broken for good. H'm! That's got rid of him! But has it? Let's move on a few years. Joseph has now risen from slavery in Egypt to be amongst the most powerful in the land. How?

26

Well, over the years, the maintenance of his life of wisdom, integrity and discernment, combined with his extraordinary gift of leadership even from within his brokenness, were recognised by those set above him. He always told the truth, even when it was uncomfortable for himself and for those who heard it. He refused to betray his master's loyalty, which would have been more common, by declining to be seduced by Potiphar's wife who then in retribution set out to discredit him and have him thrown into prison. In that place he did not waste time and creative energy defending and justifying himself, bemoaning the injustice of his fate, but from that broken place carried on dreaming and being open to God's discernment for others. So here in prison, this chosen, blessed young man was broken again that he might be given to others in that place. His jailors respected him, gave him responsibility and eventually he was freed to rise in power, trust and authority in that land where he was once a slave.

Moving on...we read where Joseph again meets with his previously scheming brothers, who did not recognise him at first. They are now poor, hungry, desperate, pleading for mercy. When they discovered his identity we read, 'They were terrified at his presence'. And here follows Joseph's struggle with forgiveness, reconciliation and mercy for those who have sought to destroy him. Yet out of his anguished struggle to do that comes the grace, even giving them the gift of permission to lift their burden of guilt. 'You did not send me here; God did, so that I might have the power to save you all now.' Joseph, chosen, blessed, broken so that he might be given to save others.

As Christians we believe likewise that Jesus was chosen blessed, broken and given; himself the gift which he brings. We too, unlikely material though we feel we may be, have been chosen, blessed, and often broken in order that we may be given for life in greater abundance. Yes, we might recognize in ourselves some of the less than noble traits of the brothers if we are honest, but, thank God, we can be 'Joseph' with his glorious coat too. But being chosen, as we have seen, entails a cost and a responsibility.

The hope and challenge is that, as long as there is a remnant, a scrap of material left, God can work with it. Trust him. He has promised. A remnant is a leftover piece. Those of us who have ever purchased remnant pieces of fabric know that with a remnant you can be extra bold; take a risk. So how do we dare to risk this scary message of refining in the fire which is so hard to hear today? Are we left with a message which says God can take away suffering, but sometimes chooses not to? Or is it that he is just not able to?

Where do questions like these, which people increasingly ask, leave us as Christians, honestly, in our own hearts? Can we believe that God does call us, the remnant into a place of suffering, brokenness or challenge, so that in and with him, we can continue to be creative and life-giving to others and ourselves? The message today might be that sometimes it just has to be like this to give mercy and truth a chance. Why do you think he has chosen you?

We began with a dream. Let's return to the image of the dream's sheaves of wheat. It comes from another spirituality pathway and was written by

27

Kahlil Gibran. It is about the redemption of pain through love. It too is about the refining in the fire. I share it in the spirit of love and hope.

Like sheaves of wheat He gathers you into himself. He threshes you to make you naked.

He sifts you to free you from your husks. He grinds you to whiteness.

He kneads you until you are pliant. And then he assigns you to his sacred fire; that you may become sacred bread for God's sacred feast.

Why do you think he has chosen you? What are the garments with which he has clothed you?

I own a model of a bust up, broken stone slab with a graffiti message. It reads, 'what remains becomes the whole'. It sits on a piece of furniture in my house to remind me. It is said that builders in past times would carve such messages one day waiting to be discovered. I have discovered the image and treasure it. What remains becomes the whole!

**

A message, a little like that of the Velveteen Rabbit that in order to become real we bear the battle scars of life... Here follows a reflection I offered at Midnight Mass one Christmas Eve after reading in Isaiah that when Jesus comes he will bring the challenge of a battle leading from darkness to light. We venture back in time into the chorister careers not of our grandsons, but of two of our sons, from a slightly alternative perspective. Enjoy!

******

Battle Garments.
Isaiah 9: 1-7a, John 1: 1-14

We have during Advent been looking more closely into our own hearts and considering that which is in darkness and longs to be brought out into God's marvellous healing light. We considered that old Beatles song about leaving one's face in a jar by the door, and about how often we wear masks, which do not show all that there is to be known about us.

Well, we all know the image of choir boys and their angelic high profile, especially at Christmas; on greetings cards, the TV, Classic FM and so on. Here is one of my diary entries from well over twenty years ago when two of my sons were choristers in Oxford...

I am writing this at one of the long refectory tables, in the dining room at Christ Church Cathedral School. All is uncharacteristically silent; the choristers have just departed into the fog, crocodile style in black hats (called berrettas) pulled low over their ears and with long woollen capes, to practise for Evensong. I reflect on the year.

William and I have walked along the river-bank, and picnicked in the summer time. Sat in the tea-shop and discussed endlessly over de-luxe hot chocolate all the matron hassles of the week. Spent numerous hours in W.H.Smith's, the favourite haunt of the choristers, where they all like to spend their pocket money. Finally, at the end of each of these precious afternoons, there is a service of peace, reflection and awe inspiring music in the Cathedral (William) or New College Chapel (Tim). The boys' singing is sublime in the true sense. The Cathedral choristers are now dressed in scarlet robes to reflect that their worship venue has a Royal charter (or black for the college choir). Around their necks are starched, brilliantly white pleated pie frills. (Who irons all those, I wonder?) Overlaying the scarlet or black vestments are white 'oversmocks' known as surplices. These little boys lead the worship, other-worldly, transporting, transforming, and transcending. Their discipline and response is instant and accurate. Their faces in the candlelight truly reflect the mystery they are but beginning to touch through their music.

Fire practice
(Drawing used by kind permission)

Can these be the same little boys who returned two hours ago, from their rugby match, covered in mud and totally unrecognisable by their nearest and dearest? Are they the same little boys who fight and hold an inquest over why Smeeton-Hargreaves is allowed seconds of custard, 'just because he has asthma and Matron spoils him'? Are they the same boys 'who shut Hermann in his trunk when they discovered there was to be a fire practice bell'? Are they those who mutter darkly that Freeman gets all the best solos probably because his Mum does the chorister teas on Fridays or even more likely because his Dad

29

is a vicar! (Actually, I heard this year that he's a vicar himself now, so all is hopefully redeemed.)

Well, yes, these are the same little boys as those who stand in church and inspire our worship, and they have much learning and growing yet to do. But it raises the paradox for me of how as adults we are all such a mixture of the light and the dark. Both are the reality of who we are, and the incarnation means the God in man embraces both the light and the dark. That is what 'incarnation' means, 'God with us'. How astonishing is that?!

Is it true that we do keep our faces in a jar by the door? Maybe Christmas time is an opportunity to review our inner hearts as well as our public faces.

Christ Church staircase

******

Chapter 2

And then the tentative schoolgirl, uniformed with satchel and shining morning face, creeping like snail unwillingly to school and intrepidly on through adolescence.

Off the Peg and Buttoned Up

1958-1967

In which I began to be a person myself and not merely one of three...the agony and the ecstasy...and when I fell passionately in love and married at twenty.

The Second Age

Naked and you clothed me
i) Changing my Clothes. The Agony and the Ecstasy!
ii) The Pinnie
iii) Matching Cherry
iv) Wearing a Swimsuit to the Office
v) Belts
vi) The White Dress from the Posh Shop
vii) In the Black
viii) The Richness of the Remnant

Naked and you called me
ix) The Remnant. Not a Treasure of the Purse, but a Treasure of the Heart
x) The Veil – Concealing, Separating or Transfiguring?
xi) My Pearls...Begin as irritants – the Gritty Components of Life

Naked and you clothed me

Changing my Clothes. The Agony and the Ecstasy!

The defining moment in the life of a young girl is the moment she is able to choose her own clothes. There are other more defining periods, menstruation, first kiss, but these are just mileposts, markers. Linda Grant

On the cusp of teenage years, with altered body image and tumultuous life changes imminent, one tentatively sets out through hitherto uncharted and stormy waters. It happened later in those days of the 50s and early 60s than today, it is true, but nevertheless...

Clothes had a lot to do with my uncertainty in those scary times. The only thing I was sure about was the need for a starched, sticky out petticoat, which my youngest sister says I paid her to starch after every wear! I think in retrospect it was probably very difficult for my gifted dressmaking mother to let go of her choices for me and throw me to the lions in making my own mistakes. (She even found a wedding dress, second-hand, for me.) Also of course we three sisters would no longer be dressed alike. We were evolving our own personas.

The agony and the ecstasy

33

As the oldest and the first to reach this stage, I encountered a difficult time until I earned my own money and was able to buy my own clothes. The more I read about the psychology of clothing, the more I understand now my confusion of those earlier times. Psychologist Flugel writes that clothes evolve like bodies, because clothes are in fact another skin. Both contemporary author Alan Bennett and more historically Laurence Sterne in Tristram Shandy, and even further back William Shakespeare (e.g. in Hamlet, *The apparel proclaims the man*) wrote around the conflict which can occur between outer and inner clothing if they are not synchronous, or reflecting of one another, and of the ensuing chaos and mayhem which can ensue. Clothing and its meaning is very important to Sterne in his exploration of what constitutes hypocrisy, especially in regard to religion.

Must the garb of religion be extended so wide to the danger of its rending, cloaked up with sermons, prayers and sacraments, yet so beautiful the externals of religion?

And in his Hezekiah's sermon, he expounds the conflict of personality garbed with a conflict of outer and inner clothing. For one of his characters, the beautiful Widow Wadman, he even leaves a blank page in Tristram Shandy in order for the reader to 'dress' her for him/herself.

The clothing theme persists throughout the book:

For Susannah the maid, *'The first thing with which to deal in a disaster is her mistress's wardrobe.'*

Then clothing metaphors abound - tenterhooks, thread, stitching, characters' shoes (*shoes change you),* and a sentimental journey will begin by *'packing a bag'.*

From Alan Bennett. Untold Stories.

He, father, had two suits, 'my suit' and 'my other suit', 'my suit' being the one he wore every day, 'my other suit' his best. On the rare occasions when he invested in a new suit, the suits moved up a place, 'my other suit' becoming 'my suit', the new suit becoming 'my other suit', with the old one just for painting or working in the [butcher's] shop. This makes him seem formal or dressed like an accountant but he did not give that impression because he never managed to be smart, his 'weskit' generally unbuttoned and showing his braces, his sleeves rolled up and when still butchering the suit would smell of meat, with the trousers and particularly the turn-ups greasy from the floor...

One day in 1970 Bennett came upon his mother with a 'stranger', someone got up in a grey check sports coat, two-tone cardigan, brown trousers and I suppose what could be called loafers. I was deeply shocked. It was Dad in leisurewear...the experiment turned out to be short–lived; soon demoted to the status of gardening clothes, and we were back on the regime of 'my suit' and 'my other suit'.

An example of needing outer clothes to reflect the integrity of the inner self for harmony!

Reminding me of my exploration historically in literature, I heard recently from one of my friends who is a volunteer support worker in an inner-city experiment to set up a protected district where sex workers are allowed to practise. Police are available to keep the area safe and there are medical helpers available for associated potential difficulties, for example, drugs, violence, drink etc. My friend, with other official volunteers, offers in a van a listening ear, hot food, and drinks for the 'girls'. She said a new van lady, in a mistaken attempt at solidarity with the girls, wore clothes like theirs, e.g. fishnet tights with holes, stilettos, enticing and revealing clothing, but she thereby unwittingly caused considerable offence to those she had come to serve. Our clothes matter.

No wonder it all seemed difficult on the clothes front! My teenage era was the Sixties and sometimes I got it right and sometimes I didn't. That was a glorious fashion explosion era, when Biba and Mary Quant were in their heyday. And yes, I did have garments of theirs eventually. A large floppy designer hat and a wrap-over, olive green jersey blouse with brown lace trim from Biba (which my tiny boobs never did justice to!). But I seem to remember as I grew to have a little money of my own that it was Wallis whence I usually trekked on my initial pilgrimage for exciting garments. One number comes especially to mind.

I reflect: It was a fuchsia pink bouclé suit with straight skirt and natty little waist length jacket with navy silk trim. Under this I wore a navy chiffon shirt which was silk lined, all except for the sleeves which showed the naked arms underneath and ended in a deep cuff with a row of tiny silk covered buttons. Goodness. What an exotic garment in which to grace my office of the Ministry of Public Buildings and Works as I ordered nuts and bolts and male and female joints and adaptors for RAF this, that and the other. 'Why male and female?' I asked my boss naively on one occasion, I recall. He was a large, florid retired Brummie policeman and somewhat astonished by my innocent question.

Nevertheless, my missed opportunity of the Sixties, from which I have never really been wholly redeemed, was life as a hippie, imagined with long plaited hair, bells on my clothes, be-sandaled or bare feet, long flowing tie-dye garb and beads everywhere! I heard very recently that the tiny mirrors on Indian fabric and clothing, which I love, have several purposes as well as being beautiful, one of which is to reflect the sun in case the wearer gets lost in the jungle!

**

But long before these independent, fashion aspirations or explorations, of course, came my secondary education. Here no deviation from the norm was tolerated in any degree...

******

The Pinnie
Written in 2015

I found new challenges at Hodge Hill Grammar School for Girls in a suburb of Birmingham. Now, unusually in the modern era, nearly sixty years later it has remained an all-girls school for a religion which does not permit girls to study alongside boys. I remember at the time my parents thought it was 'good' not to have boys there, so that I wouldn't be distracted by them when the curiosity arose. Same thing really!

It also meant that a strict uniform was compulsory, so here was another instance of my clothes being imposed upon me – no choice at all. So, did it reflect who I was inside? Of course, it did at that time. It proclaimed to the world at least that I was bright enough to have passed the 11+ exam and that my parents were prepared to make sacrifices for me to become an educated woman of the new working class, post war generation. I was to have opportunities.

The outfitter's outcome!

It meant that I consented to wear a tie (hitherto understood as something which only boys and men wore), but first I had to learn to tie it! Several Enid Blyton artefacts had to be obtained, suitably and clearly marked like everything else with Cash's name tapes, e.g. hockey stick and studded boots, games skirt (no shorter than four inches above the knee) and tennis racquet. (Oh the humiliation of all those instruments of torture over the next six years!) I had to have a school skirt of regulation length, judged by kneeling at the feet of the school outfitter till it just brushed the floor, and other unfamiliar garments, including a pudding basin felt hat held on with tight knicker elastic. Later in portentous tones in Assembly, older girls would be reprimanded for having stuffed the by now limp elastic up inside their hats, which were discovered to have been, horror of horrors, affixed to their heads (or to aspiring beehive hair styles) with Kirby

Grips! Such 'gels', if discovered to be turning to this practice, would be disciplined in future. Brown shoes only were allowed; and no nail varnish or jewellery was to be worn. 'If stockings are worn to school they should be unladdered. Any girl persistently wearing laddered stockings will be required to change into ankle socks'.

'You have been warned!'

However, I am now to speak of one item of my school uniform which was as yet not created and had to be made before I could do the lesson I was most looking forward to, cookery. It had to be crafted in my second term. By me! Oh my goodness! I was not the capable sister who was good at all this sort of sewing stuff. I had never made a felt rabbit in my life, for example, nor even a squirrel. So, for me this was a daunting prospect; and I tell you, this was to be an amazing garment, and now I realise it was an item of clothing to include just about every sewing process which existed. So one had to learn and practise these sewing skills to an acceptable standard before being allowed to cook!

The material was high quality, white linen and involved the following techniques so you will see what I mean: French Seams; Hemming Stitch; Pockets; Pleats; Tucks; Button Hole; Long Tie Belt; a Bib or Yoke; Waist Band; ah, no Zip mercifully.

Not the school pinnie!

My sister and I reflected recently that maybe these compulsory cookery pinnies were designed to keep us in our place by looking like maids and servants, should we be aspiring mistakenly to academia. Were these garments thus shaping my expectations, I now darkly speculate? Oh the misery of achieving a pinnie acceptable both to my mother and my sewing teacher. Even after that, it had to be immaculately laundered after every cookery lesson, be kept stain free and starched and most of all present and correct. No excuses like, 'I left it at the bottom of my satchel by mistake', 'My Mum didn't get round to washing that week', 'the dog was sick on it just as I was coming out'. But for those who hated cookery, sadly there was always a temporary spare, so no escape that way.

I loved cookery, but was too wildly creative at it to be a success in that class. 'Gather round gels and come and see what this silly gel has done.' Or 'What on earth are you doing trying to make vol-au-vent cases by draping uneven pastry over my best pastry cutters and putting them in that hot oven?' Of course, in working class Birmingham in the 1950s I had never seen or heard of a vol-au-vent in my life, but they sounded delicious in my Good Housekeeping cookbook when we were invited to be innovative on one isolated but glorious occasion. Humiliating times and correlating with Mrs Markwell's legendary and prophetic pronouncement (she was one of only two married members of staff in the school other than the mad science teacher, Mr Hardman): 'The root cause of Napoleon's downfall was over-ambition; he attempted too much.'

Alas Mrs Chalacombe, teacher of housewife skills extraordinaire, would never know about my Wellsprings hospitality forty years ahead, where the good news is that my cooking became a local legend in its lifetime. Traditional food, cooked on an Aga, served at a table with fine linen - though strangely no pinnie was in evidence.

My friend Bren adds, *'At my girls' Grammar School we were taught the next task (after making the pinnie) of how to make cocoa and toast for when returning home late in the evening. The warning issued to us in the middle-class Home Counties was to 'Be careful gels not to burn the cuffs of your fur coat sleeves on the gas.'*

At this point I offer into the context of this time the work of Muriel Spark, in her Prime of Miss Jean Brodie; the story of a teacher in a girls' school encouraging her pupils to look beyond 'wifehood' as a career.

This is one of the fiction works which I was allowed to borrow from the school library, once I had reached the elevated 6th Form. Re-reading this in my late sixties, here are some insights which I certainly did not have at the time. They come in the comment of an email to my fellow book group readers as I was not able to be present at a recent meeting. But clothing's close bedfellow was the significance of body shape.

I particularly noticed the changing shape of her bosom, this time when we watched the film. This was confirmed for me later in a study guide; i.e. the shape and strength and pointyness of it was significant; part of the paradox of the whole. Sometimes she was shapeless and the girls were always looking out for a change of shape in case she was pregnant. Another paradox was her strength and yet vulnerability; although she prided herself on her insight and intuition, she never even suspected the girl who betrayed her ultimately.

The notes suggested that Jean Brodie was not unique in trying to make her mark as an unmarried woman as, because of the war, many had lost potential husbands. She was unusual in that she was operating in the reactionary context of an old-fashioned boarding school whose Biblical motto of praising the wifeliness of woman being above rubies was displayed as a prompting to the girls as to their chosen destination!

She gets up while it is still dark; she provides food for her family...she makes coverings for her bed; she is clothed in fine linen and purple. Proverbs 31:15, 25

**

And now I invite you to meet my school friend, 'Matching Cherry'...

******

Matching Cherry

Quentin Crisp writes about packing clothes,
> *Don't ask yourself what is there on the outside that I want. Instead ask yourself 'what is on the inside that I need to unpack?'*

I had one really good and close friend at my Grammar School – Cherry: we remain in touch to this day.

Two of a kind

Until my teens, my mother chose my clothes but they increasingly did not 'feel me' or who I was unconsciously becoming. It meant much trauma in our house, even occasionally involving my father in controversy. Being the oldest, I paved the way in these issues for my two younger sisters. Tantrums, tears, despair. I didn't realise fully that my clothes inspiration in those days came from Cherry, to such an extent that in old photographs I observe that we were in al-

39

most identical outfits. (Just as my sisters and I had been dressed identically in earlier times.) Unbelievable really!

She seemed to me a very superior person as her parents owned a shop; she lived in a 'bought house' and was an ONLY CHILD! I could scarcely imagine the bliss of that! Also, she was 'brilliant' at art. She now says she was attracted to my whole family and particularly my parents who were much younger than hers, and because we all went to church. That aspect of our family life ultimately formed her too, as the years went on, and has subsequently become very significant in her own family life.

Two identical outfits particularly are remembered through small black and white Brownie box camera photographs: in one, Cherry and I are on the quay in Appledore in identical poses, one foot in front of the other. We wore identical cotton dresses (I think from BHS), with dropped waists and decorated with less than discreet oranges and lemons. Our heads sported identical straw flowerpot sunhats and the outfits were completed with American Tan stockings and brown leather pointed-toe sling-backs. That was on holiday with my family in Devon.

Her family always went to Barmouth in Wales and one year I went along too. This year saw the introduction into our holiday luggage of our first pairs of jeans. With these bold and grown up trousers went a grey angora, soft, short sleeved, fluffy jumper apiece. Thus identically attired one day in the sand dunes we met a rock group likewise on holiday in Barmouth, who had actually been on 'Thank your Lucky Stars'. Enough said regarding that encounter and we have lived to thank our lucky stars that we survived it...unscathed!

Along with church, clothes and dressmaking also became very significant for Cherry. For years she has had her own dressmaking studio at home and her garments are striking and immaculate. People buy them, order them, and her grown up children still love her creations. She mutters darkly that the year before M&S went big on the innovative Batwing T-shirt sleeves she had already made them for her girls and their friends!

She was always out of my league, yet we still rejoice in our friendship!

**

And, of course, into our holiday suitcases were packed tiny bikinis for very skinny girls...

******

Wearing a Swimsuit to the Office
Written in 2015

There was a hit song in the 60s, 'She wore an itsy bitsy, teeny weeny, yellow polka dot bikini'. I heard it over and over again as I served on Pick and

Mix sweets in Woolworths in the Bull Ring in Birmingham on Saturdays. Of course, I had one for myself, but without the yellow polka dots. So...

From the itsy bitsy, teeny weeny, pleated blue, nylon bikini of my youth to the more robust M and S lycra size 16, all embracing and upholding swim suit of my retirement, swimming has been the ONLY permitted exercise of my life because it is non-competitive; gentle; I can think my own thoughts while I go, and when in the sea, I imagine I could go to the edge of the horizon or even beyond.

The sadness of little breasts pervaded my early years, analogous to the small shop-bought coconut pyramids, compared with my mother's home-created giants made with condensed milk that echo my melon-like structures today which seem to believe they are feeding my five babies again, all at once. But they currently keep me well afloat in the quiet, nearby swimming pool. There I can even listen to *Spem in Alium* by Tallis, or dance to *Don't Cry for me Argentina*, as I go. That is, when I am on my own.

Nowadays, once a week I do not go on my own. I take with me some-one who for me was my administrative 'Jeeves' and much more besides, when I was Reader in Charge of three rural parishes in North Yorkshire. I can never repay her for her discreet, loyal and wise friendship. She is so special, she would not even relate to what I have just written. She and I still call this pool 'The Office'. This was where we could do all our planning, feedback, exploding in frustration etc. Here was a watery haven where we could not be overheard, interrupted or suspected of heresy. Now it is also her space in the week when she has some respite from the demands of her poorly husband. And, of course, the exercise is beneficial for the arthritis in our knees: that is until we have knee replacements, when apparently we won't be able to do breast stroke any longer.

This will be no good thing, because we don't do crawl or backstroke as we don't like getting our hair wet or even putting our faces under water; because of course we would hate to wear those swimming hats like hydrangeas, and would hardly submit to the indignity of goggles!

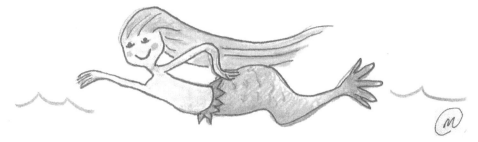

The expert!

At about the age of thirteen, a 55 bus took me to learn to swim in Woodcock Street Swimming Baths. This would be followed by chips in newspaper (six penn'orth). So from that time, through and beyond Instow Beach; South Sands at dawn; family (not Paul, who hates water) skinny dipping in a friend's private lake called Pochards, despite leeches, weeds, mud, ugh! (but it made us feel like Brideshead Revisited) and on to my current stress buster, swimming has been one of the greatest gifts and joys of my life. And now this nearby pool is an occasional watery privileged zone for my visiting grandsons - what a joy! NO running, diving or jumping though. More of a restriction for them than for me, it has to be said! Oh, and then there is Emma and Lorenzo's sun-warmed paradise pool at Casa Romanelli in Tuscany, but that is another story. 'Please don't take the inflatable friends out of the water, else they stick to the walls in the heat and then they burst.'

Paul, I understand, still carries a black and white Brownie camera photograph of me on Instow beach in the 'itsy bitsy' in his wallet (fifty years later). Today you would of course carry a Tablet or phone round with you in order to look at family snaps. In that picture I do have a racket in my hand, which is surprising as I cannot imagine I ever could have hit anything with it, but I suppose I still used to try in those days.

To finish...a fishy tail or tale:

One day the little fish went to the Queen of all fish and asked where the sea is? I have heard a lot about it but I have never seen it. The Queen of all fish said to the little fish: the sea surrounds you. You were born into it; you will die in it; it feeds and nurtures you; you will grow up in it; you will learn all there is to learn in it; you are the sea.

My hope is that, like the little fish in the sea, we are in God. We can't see him, yet He is around us; within us; we are part of God. He is part of us and He is our life and integral to our loving and learning, wherever we are on this journey of creation which is such a mystery. That is the wonder of it.

**

And so on to the belts, which hold it all together!...

******

Belts

We wore a lot of belts in our teenage years; many and varied. Was this the start of needing to be able to hold everything together?

A friend Carol, brought up in Canada, sets us off. She wrote recently:

First, for warmth we wore ribbed cotton stockings held up with garters. So, we were forever pulling them up, as they would continually fall down and ruffle around our ankles. Not very lady like! Then there were lyle stockings which always seemed to be baggy, followed by nylons held up with a suspender belt (two fasteners per leg, one of which sometimes came undone resulting in the fear of a double undoing and a sudden stocking around your ankles). Nylons had back-of-leg seams running up the calf, which a well brought up lady would endeavour to keep straight. We had to walk without rubbing our legs together as that might move the seams out of place. I was clearly not a well brought up lady and so was forever fixing things! What a relief when tights came along and seams had disappeared from them. But for a while anyway, to wear seams was a sign of superiority!

So, how interesting that Carol's comments reflect exactly how women experienced wearing seams and suspender belts (uncomfortable and a nuisance) and yet men still loved both. I have asked Paul for a quick response to this from a male point of view. He replied that it made young men contemplate the mystery of what might be revealed to them one day in the future! In the war, I understand, when nylons were not available in Britain, young women would draw a seam up the back of the leg with pencil, so those seams may have been important in contributing towards the war effort in some way indiscernible to women but helpful to the men! Enough! We move on.

Suspender belts introduce me to the memory of the battalion of belt type underwear we wore then as a routine foundation to whatever we wore on top. There were pantie girdles, to be worn over knickers for extra ballast, or roll-ons with suspenders attached. Both were constructed of firm elasticated material designed to draw in and support that which may be in danger of escaping as a sag! I do not know of anyone who still wore corsets, although I 'saw them about', so someone must have, but they too were designed to alter the lovely soft body curves underneath, via hooks, laces and even whalebones. These must yet again have been uncomfortable to the point of being excruciating and deforming and yet they too are a garment considered sexually exciting. As of

43

course are garters! In the face of all this one of my mother's favourite wisdoms was 'Men are a different species, girls'.

Bras are another sort of belt really, but holding in and up different bits of our anatomy. I lived through the Sixties and the feminist 'Burn the bras', although I didn't fully understand the political implication at the time. I just remember longing for breasts big enough to fit in one and make one wholly necessary. How that was to change a decade later as I tried to manage much larger appendages in bras like hammocks with let-down flaps in order to feed my five babies through the Seventies. That era mainly passed me by really in terms of anything which was going on outside my body and our home. And then there was of course the unmentionable, never to be discussed, sanitary belt. You were just presented with it and a huge pad but no explanation as to what happened next. These were just all the under belts. Over belts were allowed to be seen and celebrated. What they celebrated were small waists, and I did have a desirable one as a teenager. Well, with all those under belts pulling me in I would have, wouldn't I? My wedding dress was a 22-inch waist, for goodness sake!

My very special belt was the one I wore at work as an Electrocardiograph technician in Dudley Road Hospital in Birmingham in the late Sixties. This was a belt of honour, and went up in grades from pale green to emerald green and finally dark bottle green as you progressed through the ranks. It was fastened with a cool, twisty buckle and graced the uniform of a white starched overall with buttons all down the front, which had to be removed every time for washing. These buttons had a sort of loopy stalk at the back and this stalk threaded through a hole opposite the buttonhole when the overall came back from the hospital laundry. Then you had a keyring-shaped wire circle which threaded through the button stalk to secure it onto the garment. These buttons and rings were a great source of controversy if you ever found you were short of a ring or a button when the time came.

I learned much about life as well as about hearts and machines in that place, although my first task was simply to learn how to dust, even in the very high places, and as I was only 5' 2" and my senior technician about 5' 10" I was always in trouble. Following this I learned the task of packet soup making for all the grown-up technicians ready for the lunch time feast. (My mother disapproved of this on several levels, of course.) Eventually I became trustworthy and was allowed to wash off the electrolyte jelly from patients' chests and finally to operate the machine. Then I learned to read the all-important graphs, but that was much later. The defibrillating machine, nearly the size of a fire engine compared to today's natty little cases, came even later, as I rushed it through hospital corridor and basement accompanied by the flip flap of my wooden Dr Scholl sandals. (How unsuitable was that!)

But these ladies taught me about life (some were even married...how scary), about marrons glacés and liqueurs, about music and irony, as well as about medical things. We went to London on jaunts to AGMs on the Under-

44

ground and even stayed in hotels. All times of initiation for me. One girl even won a Mini in a competition with Kellogs.

I spent a wonderful afternoon with two of them recently in our late sixties, seventies and eighties. The previous time we had all three been together was fifty years earlier, we decided. Did we reminisce? A little maybe, but most of the time we still just enjoyed each other as we are today. I am thankful for these women in my life who taught me so much; especially about unsuitable 'bought' buns from the hospital canteen. Delicious! We had some at our reunion. What I have been thankful for is the knowledge in some elusive part of me, that over the many years and many miles my old friends have remained important. I have written to them once a year and that has been enough to make last month's encounter possible. In fact, my Chief technician was one of those who has most encouraged me in writing my story around the clothes we wear or don't!

I don't wear belts much of any sort now, but I still seem to be trying to hold everything together!

**

Now moving on from belts to the posh frock!...

******

The White Dress from the posh shop!
Written in 2013

The Birmingham 55 'buzz' route ran from Corporation Street in the centre of the city into Shard End Estate, on the extreme edge of the south-east side of the growing conurbation of this industrial city. You only said 'buzz' if you were 'common' which we weren't, so from now on it will be 'bus'. This blue and cream double-decker wound its way from Shard End Secondary Modern (there was no bus to my sparkly, glassy new grammar school overlooking Bromford Race Course; you just had to walk or maybe cycle), past the new shops ('tatt'), past the Raven Pub ('where the Catholics go as soon as they come out of church') - my mother's judgments and indoctrination from an early age - and so on to town, through Alum Rock, past the Saltley Gas Works and the bombed derelict HP sauce factory.

These buses were increasingly staffed by immigrants, initially Jamaican, Caribbean, shiny exotic men, with beautiful manners and lovely voices, white toothy smiles, welcoming with their hospitality as you boarded their bus. In those halcyon days, there were both driver and conductor. The driver drove and stopped; the conductor conducted, i.e. took the money, punched the tickets, gave you change without an issue, moved you along the bus and sent the smokers upstairs. No travelling on the platform was ever allowed, for your own safety. One now knows they were possibly lawyers, doctors or teachers in their own countries, coming here to make a new and better life! They seemed to me

45

to express a freedom and joy in life which was mysterious and exciting in the 'not knowing'. What has this to do with the dress?

My first clothing purchase after I earned and saved some Saturday job money (17/6p a day on the sweet counter at Woolworths in the Bull Ring) was the white broderie-anglaise dress. It had full length close fitting sleeves, and was nipped in at my 22-inch waist, and oh bliss oh joy, buttoning all down the front with wibbly wobbly, natural mother-of-pearl buttons. The cost at 6 guineas was outrageously unthinkable, requiring much deliberation and entailing a certainly never to be owned up to extravagance. My own beautiful elder daughter wore it a few times in the early Eighties and it is now with a tiny young woman whom I met through my ministry in the late Nineties when I officiated at her mother's funeral.

Back then, one Sunday morning in 1962 as I prepared to alight from the platform of the 55 at the bottom of Timberley Lane on my way to church, the gracious and glorious conductor said to me, 'Forgive me, ma'am, if I say that it is a pleasure to see a young woman in a pretty dress these days.' And yes, I did feel like the Queen!

However, my sister recalls another bus conductor more scathingly observing my trendy, grey, herringbone tweed, fitted maxi coat one day with the comment, 'The coach and horses will be along later!'

Emma reminisced recently: *I once wore the beautiful dress to a church Barn Dance and at a particularly memorable point in the proceedings, when I was do-see-do-ing with elderly Eric Overall, he swept me off my feet and swung me round so enthusiastically that ALL the buttons down the front of the dress popped open!!! And he still carried on swinging me round! Hee! Hee!*

**

That was the posh white frock and here is the black number, as experienced by my boyfriend, now my husband of fifty years…

******

In the Black

Paul reflects;

Women may think of the little black dress as just a basic item of wardrobe. But one night over fifty years ago, its seductive power blew my teenage boy's mind. And I so enjoyed the experience that I never recovered. Happily!

The 2nd World War fixed an "entrenched" mindset in the young adults who survived it. Make do and mend. And they went on to create a baby-boomer generation against a background of 1950s austerity. Then those babies reached teenage…and transformed society.

46

The hitherto all-powerful bands were gradually pushed to oblivion. Up rose the screaming, rebellious era of pop. Many roguish groups appalled parents. Their decibel levels and outlandish behaviour offended the older generation. And, in particular, convention thought their appearance unacceptably weird, and what a challenge that was to their everyday young peers too.

I well remember the agony of trying to follow the Beatles look, in their smart suits – but without lapels! I insisted one of my jackets be butchered accordingly to become on-trend, but I was too embarrassed to wear it. Even less could I have carried off the alternative long-haired look. Quite effeminate with psychedelic shirts in bright swirly colours. The hippie scene. It was a world quite alien to my boys-only, direct grant school background.

So, my fashion bravery was fated to be stilted and orthodox. Carnaby Street might as well have been a million miles away. Ninety percent of my waking hours were spent in school uniform – the only variation being a change of tie to suit the day of the week. For a few years on a Friday I made the two-bus journey to school in military CCF uniform – first army, with shiny boots and brass buckle, plus blancoed belt and gaiters, then in full naval gear with pre-trendy flared trousers. People stared and I felt very conspicuous. Maybe it subliminally nurtured my nascent patriotic pride. But above all it taught me that clothes could get you noticed.

Sunday, however, was a potential breakout day. The three visits to church were character-forming in more ways than one. The behavioural standards have perhaps never left me. But horizons widened on this, my only heady, dual-gender day of the week. Gradually a certain female infiltrated my otherwise wholly masculine world. The shapely calf was impressive. So too the clever make-up and amazingly complex hairstyles. And my smartish, staid appearance gazed in awe at those figure-hugging short dresses and skirts, trendy coats and sexy stilettos. Their irresistible appeal told me that someone desirable must reside within. And so it proved.

One memorable evening my schizophrenic lives finally overlapped. Sport was my acknowledged extra-curricular, non-academic forte, but suddenly a school dance offered the chance to bring my girlfriend out of her legendary closet and show her off to my weekday world. And the little black number that she chose to wear worked an everlasting magic on me. That night I surreptitiously stared at it to my thumping heart's content – and I'm sure others did, behind my back. But in a certain, quiet, dark classroom I got to touch it too.

The rest is history, as they say.

**

Little did he realise the eccentric variety of sources whence other clothing delights originated...

******

The Richness of the Remnant
Written in 2013

Remnants were significant in my early family life. They also, as in the Scriptures, represented treasure of the heart rather than the purse! In the Fifties and Sixties when I was growing up, in a household with a mother brilliantly accomplished in needlework, remnants of fabric were very exciting. Money was scarce, so to discover a remnant in a shop of considerable stunning design and quality for a fraction of the original price, was treasure indeed. You rooted through bins, baskets, tables and counter tops to discover them. Sometimes a whole garment could be made out of one. I have just sold such a 1950s skirt in the Vintage Clothes shop in York for £30.00! My sisters and I had patchwork bedspreads, also made by my mother from remnants of the clothes she had made over the years. There were the three new dresses, for each of the three of us every summer; so much fun on hot sleepless nights tracing them and remembering them together, as we all slept in the same room in those days. I did not inherit my mother's skill, but made some brave attempts as a young mother of five children in the Seventies, with the glorious Clothkits (you could make a pair of dungarees in an evening); but my pride and joy was crafting a pinafore dress for myself by joining patches of remnants together. And now even more patches...

These musings are prompted by helping my father sort out my Mum's wardrobe as she is becoming less able to dress herself or select her own clothes each day. You couldn't even see what was in the wardrobe as the clothes were jammed in; decades worth, family events and different eras worth, all trying hard to breathe and be celebrated.

I have spoken earlier of my mother's slenderness, such that none of the clothes of the several incarnations in her wardrobe were suitable for me and my now rather 'cuddly' size. Except for one glorious garment. Oh my goodness! There it nestled, squashed in amongst the stiff little waistbands and box pleats, kilts with tight leather straps and buckles, the Harris Tweed itchy number, and the enviable tiny Clothkits suit in peacock blue and navy slim corduroy velvet, including a natty little matching waistcoat.

Have my eyes deceived me? My mother would never have worn anything like that. It was there, languishing in all its glory, as unlikely an occupant of that wardrobe as was the Crimplene suit which hung there disconsolately. NO ONE in our family would EVER have worn Crimplene ('common').

I digress...there it was crying out, 'please release me'. Why did she make it? Whenever would she have worn it? It was not her sort of thing AT ALL, but very definitely mine! Ironically, it would still fit her as it was wrap-around. I went to the sitting room in trepidation. 'No, I'd never wear that now,' she said, 'I don't know why I made it! Yes, you can take it!' Oh bliss oh joy. What a swirl of subliminal memories. Remnants and patches and the only garment in the wardrobe to fit me. Thank you. Thank you, my lovely, creative, gifted mum!

On that black, floor-skimming, swirling, wrap-around skirt were sewn big, bright, uneven patches, many with memories for me going back decades. From my first maternity mini-dress (for goodness sake), orange flowers; several of Emma's little two, three and four year old dresses, a particular favourite was one with tiny giraffes on viyella, my maternity breast feeding nightie, navy viyella with tiny pink flowers, pearl buttons of tucked bodice, my bridesmaid dress for my younger sister's first wedding, pale blue cotton in a sculptured thread, a little pink candy-striped sun dress from when I was a child.

And yes, I did wear it straight away to William and Louise's Midsummer music concert at Bartlow on the day of the Summer Solstice this year, under the direction of his Old Etonian friend, Peter Asprey. In that tiny country church, under the Medieval wall paintings of the Angel Michael weighing the souls of the aspirants to Heaven, and suffering dragons, he conducted a small choir in works by Byrd, Britten, Rutter and Stanford, then finished with traditional English madrigals, all followed by sharing in my friend Heather's celebration chocolate fudge Midsummer cake and cool wine; after which finally we all skipped away through the woods and round the windy paths through the undergrowth as darkness fell, to arrive at the clearing in a ring of trees, where astonishingly rose the Three Hills; the burial mounds and barrows...magical!

The evocative skirt celebrated its first outing for many years; indeed a treasure of the heart, and of the love and memory of our family life: a gift from my Mum.

**

And this takes us through to my inspiration of remnant as a spiritual treasure of the heart...

******

Naked and you called me

The Remnant

'Therefore, pray for the remnant that still survives'. Isaiah: 37: 4

A remnant? A scrap of material? Remnant is an important concept in the Bible. It is one of the most significant Old Testament concepts in the Divine oversight of Hebrew history. Even when the nation as a whole deserted their faith, there remained a remnant whose faithfulness prevailed. Maybe one of our tasks today as the remnant of God's church is together to know better how to help others share that treasure of the love of God for all of creation with which we have been entrusted. This is not the treasure of the purse, but the treasure of the heart.

Simeon and Anna - Faithful Remnant of Israel.
Luke 2: 21-40

Jesus is revealed to Simeon and Anna as the promised Saviour who is able to reveal to us our true selves if we read with our eyes and ears and hearts open to the God of all creation working within us.

When Mary and Joseph brought their new baby son into the temple, here were two wise and elderly people to greet them, who had waited all their lives in the hope of this moment. Simeon and Anna had both loved God all their lives, and if any of us do that, we will also be wise and lovable in our old age. We can't truly love God all our lives and end up crabby and narrow-minded! When we spend a lot of time with another person we get to know how they think, and we understand them better and better. It is true that if we spend time with God like this, even if we only begin today, and carry on right into our old age, we will get to know him better and better, and it won't be long before we can hear when he speaks into our hearts. This is how Simeon and Anna knew that this baby was the one they were waiting for. Simeon had been told that he would see the promised Messiah in person before he died. He had been listening to God all his life and because he was used to listening to God, he was able to recognize beyond doubt the prompting that this particular baby was God's chosen one. Here they are the faithful remnant of Israel, watching and waiting with Godly living and a hopeful heart.

At first glance, Jesus would look like any other baby, and Mary and Joseph like any ordinary fairly poor set of parents, rather dusty after their journey. Jesus was carried in and recognized by those who were wise and mature in spirit. God's glory is expressed both in the awesome beauty of holiness and yet also in the immanent vulnerability of the human baby. Simeon had no problem with Jesus being the light for the whole world, but his perception also enabled him to see something of the inevitable 'suffering servant' role the Messiah will have as he reveals people to themselves. Some will find this a key to new life, whilst others will prefer to reject the light of truth. Simeon can see that an intrinsic part of saving through love and truth is making enemies and meeting conflict and suffering; suffering that this young woman, his mother, will be bound to share. This is what will happen when the Kingdom of God confronts the Kingdom of the world. Mary will look on in dismay as her son is rejected by the very city to which he has offered the way of peace, by the very people he has come to rescue. He also sees that the coming of Jesus for the whole world is not what Israel was expecting but true revelation and true glory nonetheless.

Luke warns us that here is something which might not have been expected. We read 'A sword will pierce her heart'. The story of joy is becoming a story of suffering. It now appears that God's appointed redeemer will deal with the world's suffering by entering it himself. It is interesting that in the art world around depiction of the Christmas story, the swaddling bands of Jesus can be said to prefigure his grave-clothes. Thus, another dimension is added to the whole Christmas story. So how does this become our story too?

By the time Luke's first two chapters are finished, almost all his readers will have found someone with whom to identify. We have met the older couple surprised to have a child at last. We have seen the young girl even more surprised to have a child so soon, and her faithful husband coming with her to the Temple to support her. The next section will feature Jesus' adolescent life. Here we have the old man and woman waiting their turn to die, worshipping God night and day and praying for the salvation of his people. Luke draws readers of every age and every stage of life into his picture. No matter who or where you are, the story of Jesus, from the feeding trough in Bethlehem to the empty tomb and beyond, can become our story. How is God calling or beckoning you into this narrative?

In becoming our story, it will become our vocation, our calling. Everybody has their role in God's plan. For some it will be active, obvious, working in the public eye, perhaps teaching, preaching or taking the love of God to meet the practical needs of the world and community. For others it will be away from public view, praying faithfully for God to act in fulfilment of promises. For many it will be a mixture of the two. Mary and Joseph needed Simeon and Anna at that moment; the old man and woman needed them. This interaction is for me the joy of ministry, not only what we can offer to others, but to receive in humility what is offered to us.

Where do you see yourself in this story?

**

Love one another, but make not a bond of love: Fill each other's cup but drink not from one cup... For only the hand of Life can contain your hearts. (Kahlil Gibran)

I could not have written this reflection before the age of twenty, when I married a gentle, clever, compassionate and endlessly patient man, my husband Paul. At that time his man-ness and passion and our dreams for the future beckoned me on...

******

The Veil

Whilst moving house once, I rediscovered my wedding dress. From the perspective of my middle age, it looked as if it would fit a Cindy doll! Reflecting on the veil led me to question its significance. Maybe a metaphor for the real me previously hidden, about to come to fulfilment! I confirmed the meaning of 'veil' in the Oxford Dictionary. 'A piece of more or less transparent material, which covers, conceals or separates'. So how could this metaphor of the veil offer insight into these accounts of transfiguration? This glorious, transcendental concept of God's light. Both for Moses and Jesus, this is not an energy of transformation, but the penetration by God of their very being and indeed beaming right to the heart of humanity itself. So, the veil...

Transfiguration.
Luke 9: 28-36, 2 Cor 3: 7-18

When...the Israelites saw Moses his face was radiant, and they were afraid to come near him...he gave them all the commands of the Lord... he put a veil over his face. Exodus 34: 30, 32,33

Here is an understanding of the veil as covering, concealing and separating. In this case Moses' face, bearing the light of God, is concealed and separated from the people.

Let's join Peter. He has not so much a veil over his eyes as a horse blanket. Whilst the glory of God is manifest in all its magnificence around him, he rushes around like so many of us, just wanting to do practical things.

It is easy to criticise Peter in his blundering, impetuous ways, but maybe he was just too afraid to look. The Bible says, 'He did not know what he was saying'. In my Bible, the passage before this is entitled 'Peter's confession of Christ'. 'Who do you say that I am?' Jesus asked. Peter answered, 'You are the Son of God.' Like Peter we do long to believe that Christ is the son of God, Saviour of the world. But sometimes the reality of what that might mean for us in our lives is not so clear. A veil, 'more or less transparent'. Is less transparent the safer option?

The Israelites were afraid to encounter the glory of God. The disciples couldn't really face it either. Can it be that we also draw a veil in our fear of truly encountering the risen transcendent Christ? The fear may be well founded because if we do dare to take the risk of becoming part of that glory, for sure transformation and change will disrupt and disturb our lives. Like the bridal veil, that which has remained hidden will indeed be brought to fulfilment. Is that what we are afraid of?

I am very interested in and inspired by Celtic spirituality. The Celtic way of life is very much part of their whole Trinitarian faith and being. Life for them is a journey, and the landscape of the created world is a metaphor for this pilgrimage. They recognize boundaries, bridges, crossing places, wells, springs and mountains as sacred space. They describe such space as a place where the veil is thin. A place where the invisible and the visible in oneself and God in all creation can be reconnected. At a place where the veil is thin, movement and awareness, material and spiritual, interweave in freedom, passing from one side of the veil to the other.

Pilgrims are encouraged to keep on travelling from one sacred space to another, and not to pitch camp (as Peter wanted to do). The spiritual life is a journey, not a structure. The call is not to contain this vision in our manmade shrines, but to listen to its truth as it speaks to our heart. We are encouraged by these accounts not to stay on the mountain but to return to the valleys. The veil of the temple between the sanctuary and the people was ripped apart for ever on the death of Jesus. God has now pledged a new covenant. No longer is the veil to conceal God or separate Him from the people He created. It is in the sacred space, the boundary place, where change becomes possible. Theologian Angela Tilby warns, 'Tradition is dynamic. The church must develop or die.'

Where a veil is thin, it is a transparent membrane. Do we dare to face the light? For sure when we have taken the risk of doing that, others will encounter it in us also. After all you can see through a veil either way if the light is appropriate! Saint Paul says, 'Whenever anyone turns to the Lord, in the new covenant, the veil is taken away'. We become more like him. He forgives us even in those parts where we feel undeserving of forgiveness. He loves us into forgiveness. Can we trust the promise recorded in Corinthians, 'And we who with unveiled faces all reflect the Lord's glory are being transformed into his likeness with ever increasing 'glory''?

The veil then, perhaps covering the real me, hiding me from what I could become if only I dared to face the light. Is your veil, is mine, more or less transparent?

**

Forty years on – Paul gave me some pearls. On a silent retreat, these reflections on pearls and their origin emerged from I know not where in my soul...

******

Prized as a gem you will grow me and shape me…

My Pearls

My pearls begin as irritants,
The gritty components of my life:
Rough and uncut,
Wandering by chance into the shell.
This first offered its hospitality to the oyster.
The oyster does not reject me, nor spit me out,
But refines me,
Smooths me,
Polishes me,
With the essence of its very self.
It becomes the patient host to the gritty me
So that I may fulfil whatever in me is intrinsically valuable –
Treasured and lustred not from without, but from within;
So that one day I may grace the banquet,
Where I eat less to satisfy desire
Than desire to eat that which truly satisfies.

Oh taste and see how gracious the Lord is...

Prized as a gem you will grow me and shape me, if I submit...
From the experience of constraint to an awareness of freedom,
From the emptiness of loneliness to the richness of solitude,
From the wounds of punishment to the balm of your touch.
I come empty but open,
In the name of two Trinities:
Father, Son and Holy Spirit,
And also one which speaks equally profoundly to me,
Mother, Maiden and Crone.
In the crucible of your shell of love,
Transform my fear into courage,
My despair into hope,
The ordinary into the extraordinary,
So that at last,
The wolf within
Is learning
To lie down
With the lamb.

******

55

Life is not about waiting for the storm to pass.
It's about learning to dance in the rain. (Vivian Greene)

56

Chapter 3

And then the elegant lover sighing like furnace, and with gentle mother's woven ballad.

Poppers, Flaps and Loose Threads

1968 - 1980

In which I became a mother of five children...fulltime housewife, almost unconscious with exhaustion day after day...appeared on BBC TV...lived in Northamptonshire and Buckinghamshire...began an Open University degree in my spare time!

The Third Age

Naked and you clothed me
i)   ...in a shoe
ii)   My Clothing of the Seventies
iii)   The Patchwork Dress and Headscarf/Sarong!
iv)   The Airing Cupboard and the Angels
v)   Contextual Theology of the Socks
vi)   Clothkits and the Open University
vii)   The Little Mary Quant Number goes to the B.B.C
viii)   Laura Ashley
ix)   Grandma's Jumper
x)   Mea Culpa

Naked and you called me
xi)   Babette's Feast. From meagre living and meeting people where they are, gently and non-threatening to an abundant banquet which transforms lives and community.
xii)   Dress Non-Sense?
xiii)   Harry and the Cloak
xiv)   The Midwife

Naked and you clothed me

...in a Shoe

Nothing prepared me for motherhood and my first baby, except the hormones, and they did not really help most of the time except to help provide my baby's food! I was many miles from my own mother, mother-in-law and any friend. We lived in a semi-detached bungalow on a new, privately built estate in Northamptonshire. Paul was out for many hours in every day as a sales representative for a major publisher. I arrived home from ten days in hospital, with a yellowish (jaundiced) but beautiful baby girl, amidst absolute fear and trepidation. Nor had anything prepared me for the total exhaustion of feeding a baby through the night and day. My mother told me that my husband was not to be disturbed at night because he had to work all the next day.

What was it I did all day? I can't be sure. In retrospect I think I must have had some postnatal depression. I know that one evening I had a hallucination that I actually saw my new baby open the sitting room door and come through. She had on her pink all in one baby-gro with poppers. The next thing I remember was changing her nappy on a changing mat and then feeding her. But that moment of seeing her open and walk round the door is as real today as it was then. That was dear Emma, always an unusual child. She says now that she remembers being in her large, coach built pram, sitting up and looking out at all the grownups, wondering why they treated her and spoke to her as if she were a baby.

I went on to have five children and eventually was known by neighbours as 'The Old Woman who lived in a Shoe'. Of course, I did get used to the motherhood business as far as one ever can, and it did become easier in that my only aim eventually was to have all five still alive, fed, clean, having had a story read and in bed at the end of every day. Then I went to bed too. But in retrospect I am thankful and privileged that I was able to be a mum at home for 20 years and for that to be my full-time job. It was wonderful, challenging, exhausting, exciting, anxiety–making, frustrating, bewildering, joyful, painful, and with many, many adventures on the way. Many loose threads abounded in this tapestry weave of our family life, certainly! Perhaps one of these loose threads was my spirituality and calling to ministry in those tumultuous times. There was no time or energy for active faith walking, although I did sit in pews as and when I could; not skulking at the back with my five children, but at the front where they could see what was going on. I was just there and that was all I could be for then.

**

But first, let us return to the clothes horse. What did I wear in these motherhood years?...

******

My Clothing of the Seventies

Happily, I could wear what I liked as I was a full-time housewife and mother and hadn't much of a clue about what was going on outside our home, other than church and parents' evenings. Well, and Waitrose. Amongst these eccentric garments were:

i)   For 'best' I would wear a closely fitting, collarless black velvet Laura Ashley jacket, with tiny velvet-covered buttons. This teamed up with a peasant long velvet multi-coloured tie dye skirt with a handkerchief hem, this latter which I still wear actually. It did originally have tiny bells sewn on too. A broad leather belt, boots and jumper completed this exotic outfit.

ii)   My wide-flared denim post-maternity dungarees with the helpful let-down flap!

iii)   A Mary Quant dress worn for a Pebble Mill T.V. experience. This was mid-calf in length on a yoke in a liberty lawn fabric with cotton lace trim and long sleeves. It had some sort of fault in the fabric which was how this prestigious garment came to be mine.

iv)   The olive-green Biba blouse, which never entirely lost its sense and smell of the clothes shop whence it was bought on only my second ever trip to London.

v)   The homemade pinafore dress sewn out of patches, now worn by my niece, the headscarf to which, having now become a sarong, is worn by Emma in the blazing sun of Tuscany.

60

vi)   Maxi coats. My favourite was the one referred to in the preface. This was actually originally what was known as a coatdress, fashionable in those times. That meant, however, that it had to go on over one's head every time. This was not very convenient for my swirly hairstyle with large black bow at the back. So, my mother slit it up the middle at the front and we made button holes and sewed on buttons. Perfect in green herringbone tweed, I wore it for years to push prams in, and it finished its life lining the cat basket next to the Aga for a litter of kittens.

vii)   Mini-skirts various, usually only in summer: for winter with boots.

viii)   A crushed loganberry-coloured velvet hat, lined with ticking, from one of those patchouli-smelling Aladdin's Cave type shops in Oxford.

ix)   I even had a hooped petticoat to wear under my Laura Ashley ball dress! This was something, I realise now, that Cinderella might have worn for a special occasion. It had a wide full-length sweeping skirt in cornflower-blue glazed cotton with many swags and bows. I wore this first in Aviemore for a Booksellers' Conference and later for a notable Midsummer soirée.

x)   My eclectic taste ran also to Hot Pants, which were a sort of shorts with a bib.

xi)   Dressed alike in the early Seventies, a young woman and I met in the village playground with our infants. She was in every way on a different experiential and intellectual planet from me, but we recognised each other from our clothes, even then unusual for the time. It began a life-long friendship across the miles and the years. I recall that we both wore huge Steeleye Span-type sunhats with flowing ribbons, long cotton print skirts and cheesecloth smocks in which we pushed our toddlers on swings, roundabout and see-saw.

All around my hat…

61

xii)   I remember a shiny cornflower-blue dress (a bit art deco) from Richard Shops, in which I felt smart and 'un-mumsy'.

xiii)   A cheesecloth top with cotton lace trim and batwing sleeves was a special summer favourite for years.

xiv)   A member of this wardrobe was an extravagant blue floral three-tiered number which I wore to push Jeremy in his pram in Towcester. I recently sold that in a York vintage clothes shop. I understand that it was bought by a student for her 'Prom' dress.

It all seems rather weird in retrospect, I suppose. A little later I took a friend from Dunstable with me to Oxford when Tim and Will were choristers. We went into the glorious eccentric clothes shops; like wonderland for me. She re-marked that now she understood where all my wacky clothes had come from. Was it all a subconscious rebellion, I wonder, from the restricted early teenage years? Certainly, in terms of spirituality, all these garments did reflect who I was inside, for better or worse!

I do remember my last extravagant purchase of a dress from a shop just after my second child was born. I only 'let it go' within the last ten years to my niece. The quality of it was exceptionally sound as usual from Wallis. The fabric was tweedy dark red with a fine cream diamond thread pattern, partially lined with a red silky material. It was full length with buttons down the length of the front for all the right reasons! With my hair up in coils, I probably imagined I was some grand Victorian lady, with my high-necked blouses beneath this glori-ous garment! You could have seen it on the washing line, although the truth was it was dry clean only, i.e. not at all practical.

**

I read recently that this type of personal memories book can either shed fresh light back through a 'window on the time', or the earlier time itself provides the window through which the memories are glimpsed - oral history. Perhaps you can eventually decide which it is. But meanwhile one dress has its own special story...

******

The Patchwork Dress and Headscarf/Sarong!
Written in 2013

I begin with a recent email from Emma in Riparbella, Tuscany:
It is HOT HOT HOT here this week in Tuscany and your gorgeous headscarf is forming the 'itsy-bitsy' foundation stone to my 'cool-as-a-cucumber' wardrobe!! Love and sartorial elegance! X

Whilst we lived in Cheddington in 1976, the country had just about the hottest summer on record. Instead of leaves hanging from the silver birch trees outside our neo-Georgian semi were festoons of caterpillars, having in desperation gorged overnight all the foliage. Great chasms appeared in the ground as cracks split up all the lawns and earthen places. Crops were lost; plants and people shrivelled in the excruciating heat. Emma and Jeremy mostly wore no clothes (knickers excepting) unless they went out (naturally), and spent day after day in their paddling pool, trying to keep cool. The day the rains eventually came after weeks and weeks, we all ran out onto the scorched 'what used to be the lawn' and stood and drenched ourselves in it. This was all before Global Warming, of course. It is very different now! Last year at York Crematorium the attendant commented to me scathingly of the Yorkshire summers of late, 'Summer? Huh! It were Tuesdee!'

Throughout this particularly tropical summer I was pregnant, and in those days the bulge was less celebrated than disguised, so I had to be very creative indeed. I made a full length maxi pinafore dress, with matching headscarf bandanna. (Why a headscarf in a heat wave? I know now.) But this pinafore dress was no ordinary garment, because it was made out of patches of designer fabrics. So first, I had to sew together all the patches, before I cut the pattern of the dress out. These patches came from a good friend indeed. This friend, who was a very holy lady in the true sense, was more experienced in motherhood and sewing than myself and kept us all on the straight and narrow in those days. She gave me her mother's beautiful painted and gilded old Singer sewing machine with which to develop my dress making skills. Her gifts included, during this halcyon clement weather, giving me a break by having Jeremy and Emma to stay overnight in tents in their garden. Sadly, Jeremy pitched his on an ants' nest, so he does not have happy memories of that occasion.

P.S. From Emma's Email: *Critical information re the ants' nest debacle - and an early indication of Jeremy's imaginary destiny as the 'Lord of Misfortune' - is that this particular balmy Summer's Eve was the one the ants chose to make their flight for freedom! Poor Jeremy! Luckily 'there was room in my tent for two'.*

This lady and her husband whom I will call Martha and Mark for the purpose of these reflections, are those whom I have to thank humbly for keeping my faith, hope and 'calling' alive through these years, in a busy little Baptist Church in Hertfordshire. Here my nonconformist roots of the Priesthood of all Believers were watered and nurtured slowly; and in the relative darkness of fallow ground I did once ask Mark to suggest any course I might undertake to exercise my dormant spiritual muscles and he did come up with one possibility, but sadly just as I became 'with child' yet again. Eventually it was through the Anglican Church that I took up an official exploration of my almost life-long calling to ministry, but more of that later.

I digress...

I lived all summer in that exotic, belatedly hippie dress. It went to picnics, church, clinics, maternity appointments, shopping, visits to my parents ('where have we gone wrong with our Ann, Bert?'). I treasured it. I still do, though it now lives with my niece. Well, the dress does. What about the bandanna or headscarf? Well, now I know why I made it in the far-off Seventies heat wave. Emma today wraps it round her slender fragile body. She takes such delight in remembering the outfit that the headscarf has now become for her a sarong! And yes, she is that tiny. It was only a little scarf after all. But she is a legend in her life-time in it, as in virtually every other way too. And then I saw its 'cousin' at an Yves St. Laurent exhibition recently…

**

But the scale of the clothing situation for the growing family could become overwhelming and it did…

******

The Airing Cupboard and the Angels
Written in 2015

The airing cupboard is the place where I finally acknowledged that I could go no further. My Waterloo! These are the days before tumble dryers, it must be noted. Where did I turn for help? I didn't – it came to me. She has been there ever since, in a miscellany of generous ways, even though a remote enigmatic figure in my life to some degree.

This 'airing cupboard' marking post in my journey of motherhood was at a time when my fifth baby, William, had recently been born in Wingrave, Buckinghamshire, when his nearest sibling Tim was nineteen months old, unable as yet to walk and still in terry towelling nappies. Emma was ten, Jeremy eight, and Hannah four. These older three just carried on in survival mode, bless them. One day, poor Hannah in her red gingham dress patiently waited for ages at the post box across the road, knowing that she mustn't cross on her own. I had forgotten to look out for her. Deadlines were a huge pressure, especially in the morning with two children having to be up and dressed for school and one for playgroup in the other direction. There was no car. Five children to be washed, dressed, fed, ready and out by 8.45am; one in the pram; one on the pram; one on reins hanging on to the pram and two walking, running or skipping along behind. Oh, I had to be dressed as well, naturally! In my role as The Old Woman who lived in a Shoe, one year I even made Emma such a themed birthday cake with two chocolate swiss rolls (home baked) set at right angles to each other, liquorice boot laces and a Shredded Wheat thatched roof!

However, the day came after about three weeks when I reached home from this daily expedition, opened the airing cupboard and saw it piled to the ceiling with clothes for seven people; weeks of washing and ironing and enough terry nappies to swaddle an army and no, I couldn't empty it. I sank to my knees in despair. I couldn't even begin to consider emptying it, sorting it into piles and putting them all away. No, that was it. I had come to the end of the line. The state of the clothes in the airing cupboard reflected what I was like inside myself, out of control but desperately trying to hang on in there, like the boy with his finger in the hole of the dyke.

Then the angels began to arrive. Tim, my beautiful little fourth child of the radiant smile, was found crawling down the main street and was returned to me by a driver who had narrowly missed driving his car over him. One of the older children's friends had left the front door ajar while I was feeding the baby upstairs. My angel in disguise was not critical or judgemental, but asked 'what can I do to help?' That day one of the mums took little Tim for the daytimes to be with his chum, Ben. Others took the three older ones to and from school. Someone must have done the washing too. Food was organised and just appeared, and all this so manifest to me as a gift without price; for a while I just went to bed with the baby each day until a baffled Paul came home from London.

When my gifted, gracious elder daughter was diagnosed at nineteen with Leukaemia, with possibly only a week to live, my angel in disguise was there in the months to come, recognising that I needed a break. Later still when we suffered a mid-life financial crisis, she was still there in concern, care and offer of accommodation for a holiday.

Very recently, the year my father-in-law died, my mother died and Paul had a malignant cancer behind his eye, she was there, offered what she could and was insightful enough each time to know just what would help.

To this day, all that has helped me always to be thankful for and to be able to recognise the angels who come gently and quietly unawares.

**

And one item, amidst that chaotic airing cupboard, created its own unique problem...

******

Contextual Theology of the Socks
(Finding God in the context of everyday life and work.)

My parents' relationship began and happened because of socks. My mother knitted them for a serviceman, away in the war. He was the son of one of my maternal grandmother's milk round colleagues. Eventually through this milky connection the owner of the socks fell in love with the knitter, and that is where this story began.

But as a mother of five children and a mystified husband, lost socks became a terrible issue in my family. The washing machine quite obviously ate them. Everyone became frustrated and did not believe me that I didn't throw them away, or that I wasn't careless with them in some way. What were they to do with 37 odd socks? I then began to rebel and refused to put them all in pairs after the washing monster had eaten them. (Bear in mind that might be 12 socks a day, or 84 in a week!) It was The Big Issue in those days! So I just began to stuff them in a big heap in the airing cupboard for owners to sort out themselves, and everyone became crosser and crosser.

One weekend, which in fact changed my life, I went away on a retreat, on my own...oh the joy and grace of others to enable me to do this. What could I do on my return to thank my husband for encouraging me to go? He had looked after all the children so that this could happen. He is a wise man obviously! Because, yes you have guessed; I tackled the socks issue in a loving instead of an angry way. Paul's comment is that they still tended to disappear, but not so many or so often!

That retreat and the introduction to contemplative prayer did change my life and rekindle the flickering flame of my calling to serve in formal ministry. It helped me also to be more aware of God in my everyday life, family and work.

From our Hertfordshire Baptist Church, we moved to worship in an Anglican church for the first time. This was because Jeremy was 'spotted' at his school by the choirmaster at Dunstable Priory. So we all went there to worship in order to transport and support him in that place! From a plain building of nonconformist tradition where the minster just preached and led worship in a smart suit, we had entered a place of sumptuous decoration and ancient lineage, whose front door bore the bullet holes of an historic incident and memories of the dissolution of the monasteries. It was in this sacred building that Thomas Wolsey announced the annulment of King Henry VIIIs' first marriage to Catherine of Aragon. In retrospect I confess that I was maybe seduced by all this setting, encapsulating the transcendental and sublime music which I began to feel I had longed for all my life, without knowing it. It was a backdrop for the candlelight, robes and powerful liturgy. But it was of the contemplative prayer that I wanted to know, experience and learn more. Ironically, it was this move to Anglicanism which has set the tone for much of the pattern and defining of our family life since. Jeremy was first a chorister here and then Tim and Will, followed even by myself! Tim and Will eventually went to choir schools in Oxford and Jeremy's two sons are now choristers in the Catholic Westminster Cathedral. Eventually I trained to be a Reader, a lay minister in the Anglican Church, and thus began several pioneering adventures, as you will encounter in these pages.

We seem to have come a long way from the socks, but it is all theology anyway!

**

So from socks and theology, here comes the innovative Clothkits revolution for busy Mums on a budget! (...The Family Allowance book was more than a comfort. The woman in the Post Office...used to stamp it, and hand over the cash, and I felt rich. Margaret Drabble. The Pure Gold Baby)...

****

Clothkits and The Open University

Clothkits entered my life, causing a frenzy of passion and activity which I had never hitherto experienced in the realm of sewing and dressmaking! This company marketed their wares in a catalogue of stunning designs in an original and mould-breaking fashion.

You did not have to mess about with floppy paper patterns which ripped and creased. Here they all were, one garment printed onto a piece of fabric, with all the bits and bobs you needed to finish them off. The thread, zips, ribbon, buckles, buttons, poppers, and then a popping tool even with which to affix them. All you needed was a pair of scissors and a sewing machine. One could make a garment in an evening - anything from dungarees, skirts, dresses, 'costumes', satchels, pinafore dresses. It felt like an exclusive club almost, and if you encountered other children and mums in these garments you knew there would be an almost instant 'recognition'. They would be printed on a variety of fabric depending on the time of year to be worn, from cord to light cotton with innovative design of another culture, natural plant and berry, fun for children or regular and irregular pattern of shape and form. My most memorable such recognition was meeting my tutor counsellor for The Open University for the first time. This would be 1980 after the birth of William, my fifth child, when I began my OU degree. I turned up in the identical peacock and royal blue cord pinafore dress to Anna, also a mother of five. Ever since we have remained close and trusted friends, clearly on the same wavelength.

I was the sort of student the OU was designed for, having stopped academic study before A levels, yet capable of doing so much more. The OU and Anna changed my life. Together they re-introduced me to art, music, literature, philosophy, social sciences and (perish the thought) even feminism in Women's Changing Experience. I was not popular on that Summer school as a mother of five children and full-time housewife, and a Christian even. That scathing tutor remarked to me, 'There is always one in a group and this week it is you.' Everyone burst long pink balloons on the last day and I just did not get it at that time. Anna steered me through.

The method of study made such sense to me after always failing to achieve fully at school. We studied not as separate disciplines, but as periods of history, e.g. the 18th Century and its art, history, music, philosophy, architecture, literature, all of that period. I could see at last how it all related and joined up, with each part reflecting the whole, so that all became greater than the sum of its parts.

I pressed on for six years, learning to read, write, reflect and 'look' again. With five small children I had to do this academic work at 5.00am before they all woke up and needed getting off to school etc. That saved me from having to marginalise them during the time they were awake. To be honest it changed the course of my life in more ways than one. I still do this kind of work, sermons and the like, although now on computer, in the early hours, leaving my days free for 'people'. But I still go to bed as soon as I can in the evening! I like to think I am like the animals and birds in that way! Works well for me, but it means I have never been effective later on at evening meetings or indeed any such event!

**

From Clothkits we return to another garment on its most public outing...

******

The Little Mary Quant Number goes to the BBC

The telephone rings one summer lunch time in the early 1970s.

This is the BBC and we are wondering if you could come into the studio to Pebble Mill at One next week and demonstrate your competition recipe live on the programme.

There must be a mistake I thought, or it is a joke?

Cooking could be interesting and confusing in those 'woman who lived in a shoe days', especially when Paul had an allotment with his harvests! There was the year when I had cooked half a pig's head for economy reasons, then drained off all the beautiful stock down the sink and was just left with the gristly bones and flabby skin. Then after the purple harvest, by mistake I made a beetroot cheesecake and blackberry soup. You would not think it possible; but it was. Economy did drive these culinary tasks. Emma remembered that she always knew if we were short of money when the lentils she usually used for collage work suddenly found their way into lentil soup. Into this context came a phone call as above.

There had recently been a competition for submitting recipes on that lunch time, pre-Watch with Mother programme, with the challenge, 'Please send in your original recipe for a meal for a family of four costing in total £1.00 or less'. 'You haven't won,' they said, 'but you are one of a handful out of over 500 submitted this first week, who hasn't used mince!'

Twenty–five years later, I re-appeared on the anniversary page of the Leighton Buzzard Gazette as having dared to do this very scary thing using fennel and cauliflower, with bacon and cheese sauce – one demonstrated live on air, followed by, bingo! Open the oven door and, 'Here is one I made earlier.'

Seeing myself on the history page reminded me that at the time, even scarier than the prospect of cooking on live TV, was the issue of 'What shall I wear?' There were only two options; a Fine Feathers Liberty viyella number with fine cord trimming and little cord-covered buttons and loops down to the waist, or my Mary Quant Liberty fine lawn tiny floral print, garnished with cotton lace round yoke and hem. You have met this earlier! Mercifully I went for the latter; merciful because Dana, the star folk singer, and later an Irish politician, also appearing on that edition of Pebble Mill, was wearing the identical Fine Feathers dress to mine! Phew! A very close shave indeed, which she will never know! Which of us would have been the more astonished, I wonder, had that been my

68

choice too? My homecoming established that Emma and Jeremy had been totally unimpressed by me on TV. They were just patiently awaiting Andy Pandy in his blue and white stripy outfit.

**

Another Sixties designer whose garments I adored in the last year of that decade was of course Laura Ashley...

******

Laura Ashley
Written in 2013

I rarely read magazines. I have virtually never sent for anything promoted in one, but on this occasion, I must have known a good thing when I saw it, early in 1970, in one of the colour Sunday newspaper supplements. In an article illustrating innovative maternity clothing, I saw the dress of my dreams; floor length, blue printed cotton with a tiny pleated bodice, from which fell the full skirt to accommodate evolving Emma. It had long sleeves and high neck, both trimmed with cotton lace (the neck looking much like a pie frill). It was designed to celebrate, not disguise or conceal, the burgeoning new life growing beneath its folds, a radical concept in that era. In it I could move as if I were a Jane Austen heroine!

Welcome to my life, Laura Ashley - who has remained significant for me for special occasions ever since, reaching her sumptuous zenith years later in the hooped petticoat foundation under the soft and silky cotton garment in cornflower blue, which I wore to the ball at the Booksellers Conference in Aveimore. (H'm! Vague stirrings of a certain Radio 4 programme accost me at this point.) There followed a significant night of passion and intrigue. My Mum and Dad were at that ball too, so it was really all OK! (as, like Paul, they were by now booksellers too). Laura Ashley continued to accompany me for many further years and in many guises – as a natty little black velvet fitted jacket; a striking blue pin-striped silky dress with boned bodice, an embroidered cream silk waistcoat (a gift from Emma); my long black dress for Emma's wedding. I wore it with a full length black velvet cloak, white fur hood and muff. Truly exotic. (Once I was a Reader this dress doubled as a cassock for a time for the reading of BCP Evensong, without the trimmings, naturally!) Emma's wedding was memorable, with Lorenzo's mother having organized it from start to finish in about three days, finally reflecting on my Bible reading on the nature of true love, as ' I have never heard 1 Corinthians 13 read quite like that before.'

This reminds me of another totally bizarre choice for Hannah's wedding which I bought from an Arab souk in Jerusalem. (Not Laura Ashley!) I still love it! And have worn it for celebrating marriage blessings, in wood, garden and by a river! In cream linen richly embroidered with cream thread, it comprises a full-length robe, with tiny linen covered buttons and stand up collar, over which is worn a full-length billowing coat, equally lavishly embroidered. A good investment then, for a heavily bartered price!

**

And now, more modestly, knitted jumpers...

******

Grandma's Jumper
Written in 2015

Kate, one of my nieces, has had such joy from inheriting one of Mum's jumpers this year. Jane writes; *She's always in it and doesn't want to wash it, as 'It won't smell of Grandma any more.'*

The jumper is in a turquoise wool with some angora, knitted beautifully by Mum, in a challenging but regular pattern. Kate wears it on top of her Breton T - shirts, under her dungarees. She says that all her friends love it and even the teenagers at Church comment. Possibly, I think, because she looks positively glowing when she wears it, which is, as I've said, nearly all the time at the moment.

She has, however, had to wash it eventually and has felt very sad. Nonetheless, it hasn't stopped her wearing it regularly and it still retains its magic.

And from Emma in Tuscany:

I am still grinning after our happy call! So hilarious to share a certain 'remembering' with you! A boyfriend had come back with me after school to 'help with' (!) my maths homework and we were all sitting down for supper when out of the blue Will candidly informed him that I vacuumed my bedroom with no clothes on! He didn't know where to look!! Hee! Hee! Funny to think that he is now an exceedingly well-respected columnist and contributor for one of the top newspapers in the country!

And I have been thinking about our story times forty years ago. Do you remember the almost unbearably poignant Borka the goose with no feathers and how his mother knitted him a jumper to keep him warm? It made me think of our prickly 'Grandma jumpers' when we were small and how perhaps her perpetual knitting was her way of wrapping us all up in her love and her wish to keep us safe and warm…

**

And yet, yes, sometimes as parents we do get it wrong...

******

70

Mea Culpa
Written in 2015

I asked my sons if they had any particular childhood clothes story memories and I am sad to say that two of them mentioned what have remained burning issues for them (I could tell by their swiftly fierce responses). There were obviously particular occasions when I got it severely wrong.

As a parent you get letters - many, many letters - from schools, with all variety of instructions, rules and events. At this time, I had five children at five different schools in three different counties, and yes, things did get mixed up. I was always under pressure and I did make mistakes. One day, Tim was to go to Oxford in his school holidays for a day choir rehearsal at New College School. I had lost the letter! He assured me he was to wear mufti, and I should have trusted him but I didn't and sent him in his uniform. This condemned him to change into and wear the choirmaster's son's clothes all day and even now I find it hard to forgive myself. The second trauma concerns having made a pair of dungarees for Jeremy, my four-year-old son, without flies in them. I don't think he has ever forgiven me, never mind my forgiving myself. As well as clothes being very central to life in those days for me, as I had to clothe five of them for better or worse on a budget, but in meal times and food, I made mistakes there too; e.g. the bullets remaining in the rabbit which I served up as chicken casserole! Meal times came around with relentless regularity. As five children, they all felt deprived as they had to share a banana between two at least and certainly there were no bags of crisps between meals. They all would have preferred the white plastic sliced bread which they had at friends' houses, to the home-made bread we made together with stone ground flour from the mill. A few tense moments! But eating together around the table full of people, family, friends and in later days, strangers too was so important.

A late addition to this work is a word from William about his uniform at a school which, it has to be said, was not his personal first choice, but they wanted him enough to offer him a virtually full scholarship, to include even payment of laundry bills!

Hi Mum, Sorry for not having got back to you about this before now. That is mostly because I haven't ever really thought about this much. Except to say wearing something that very few owned and even fewer knew how to put on did add to the air of exceptionalism one felt right from the moment you put it on in the morning to the moment you took it off in the evening.

**

As a young mum and outside caterer, Ann's Pantry, with one of the tools of my trade

I digress – feasting – I wrote a reflection on a rather 'alternative' film I had the privilege to see once and have never forgotten. A young woman came battling through a torrential storm, a refugee in a strange land, clothes soaking wet and near the point of death...

******

72

Naked and you called me

Babette's Feast
Luke 14: 15-24, 2 Thess. 2: 1-5, 13-17

"When you give a banquet, invite the poor... and you will be blessed."

I'm going to tell you the story of a film about another banquet called Babette's Feast. This reflection was written to give food for thought as we approached Advent one year in the parishes. Advent, this time when we begin to consider more closely what is going on in our hearts, in our lives, in what motivates our way of life, our relationships with ourselves, one another and with Jesus Christ.

Here is a parable of a community; Godly people who welcomed a stranger, a refugee, into their midst, and thereby became transformed. It is a parable about movement in quality of hospitality; the welcoming of the stranger, who in turn became the host and through which transformation became possible. The good news for us ordinary people is that this transformation happened around an ordinary table...a situation not beyond any of us. It is a parable which reminds us that we are not here today because we are wonderful people, but because God can use us as ordinary people to do wonderful things for him. Babette's Feast, set at the end of the late 1800s, takes place in a fishing village on a harsh and lonely coast in Denmark. It is a Lutheran community which is shaped by the pastor. Dressed in the plain black and white of the Puritan, not exactly tyrannical but clearly in charge, this pastor and his Lutheran pietism dominate the community ethos. Most evident is his control over the lives of his two lovely daughters, calling them the 'left and right hands of my ministry'. They became in due course ageing maiden ladies, impoverished themselves, but continuing their lifelong practice of care for the really destitute of the village. Taking simple food for the hungry, like this parable of Jesus, feeding those who could never repay them.

One night, during a horrendous storm, into their humble dwelling stumbles Babette, weak, clothes soaking wet, hungry, nearing collapse. She is fleeing from Paris after a revolution. Homeless and penniless, and speaking no Danish, she is welcomed into their home, and takes over the household chores, especially in the kitchen. What we do not know then, but learn later, is that she has been the crème de la crème chef at a 5-star Parisian restaurant. So even the village poor, with their steady diet of smoked dried lute-fish and common gruel, notice that their simple meals improve.

Fourteen years go by. Even though the old pastor is dead, they carry on his Puritan regime. Long solemn prayer meetings continue around his old table, over which still hangs his sombre portrait. They speak of him reverently and continually; and yet...despite their religious piety the village is now fairly dysfunctional. There are longstanding feuds. People, who will not forgive each

73

other, bear grudges, gossip about one another. Into this situation Babette receives a letter from Paris. One of her aristocratic relatives back in France has been buying her a lottery ticket ever since she had to leave and we learn that she has won 10,000 francs, a fortune for those days. She goes off to the dunes to meditate and pray, and returns asking if she can put on a feast for the whole village, with her own money. They object, as feasting is not part of their Puritan religion, but she convinces them and goes to work. We see a boat arrive from France and a procession carrying all the food, including a live turtle comes on a wagon load up the beach, with many villagers helping to bear this to the kitchen.

When the day arrives, the villagers are very uncomfortable and do not want to enjoy this feast, in case their souls suffer damage. The grace they pray is 'Dear Lord. Please take our sense of taste away that we do not enjoy this feast.' Yet as the feast goes on and course after course arrives with appropriate wine accompaniment, borne by a young villager whilst Babette remains unseen in the kitchen, things begin to change. Most notable is the change in conversation as lifelong pietists shed their veneers and begin to confess their sins to one another and to be forgiven by their victims. Hatred, adultery, theft, untruth, false humility, to name but a few. Towards the end a guest stands up and quotes the old pastor's favourite Bible passage from Psalm 85, 'Mercy and Truth are met together; righteousness and peace have kissed each other'. We know these words have become true for the fading lives around that table.

Babette became the agent for transforming these pious Lutherans into graced and truthed Christians. She had given her all for these people. Her feast worked wonders. The guests leave the feast arm in arm, reconciled, transformed. Yet this parable-film is not about Babette, a French woman. It is a metaphor for Christ. Jesus Christ, the guest at his own feast if we invite him in; himself becoming the host. He himself is the feast which he brings. Where will we find him? It tells us here.

"When you give a banquet, invite the poor...you will be blessed."

"Go out to the roads and country lanes and make them come in."

I reminded the congregation that day that we were not there because we are wonderful people, but because God can do wonderful things through us too.

In some ways, this story offers a preview lesson for the decades of my life to come. First it prefigured my calling to use our Bedfordshire home as a retreat centre, Wellsprings, a place of hospitality to those of any faith or none. Its work indeed built up around abundance, open-ness and the 'feast' on the table!

Secondly, it inspired one of the most rewarding events in my time as a minister. From Wellsprings I moved north to three rural Yorkshire parishes. One year we held such a feast in our village. The church could not agree on what the charge for it should be. Some said people would not pay for something the church put on. Some said only if you charged a great deal would people think it was worth it! No one would come anyway, they predicted. In the end I advertised it free of charge. I would do the cooking and provide the food. Someone gave their house as a venue. About forty villagers turned up and sat around the table, those who had served in the past, alongside those who had hitherto been

74

served! A very wonderful occasion and on the way out, people threw money with abandon into a bowl in thanksgiving!

**

Babette did not try to out-do this community or undermine them in any way, even from her great experience and skill. She earned their trust of her patience. Quality of taste is important in this story. Taste in the choice of our clothing is part of the adventure of our God-given humanity. Some maybe no longer have the option of choice…

******

Dress Non-Sense
Matthew 22: 9

A few years ago, whilst still in my Anglican ministry, I was in a local church for a licensing service for new Readers. It was packed full of visitors from all over the diocese. The organ was marvellous; the choir excellent. The Bishop was magnificently attired in glorious scarlet and dozens of Readers in orderly pairs processed graciously in their robes. The Church of England do this sort of thing well and ritual is certainly an important part of being human.

I had to leave early and, sitting on a bench outside waiting for a lift, I was joined by a battered-looking man; shabby of dress, slurred of speech, vacant of eye, and unsteady of foot. He took a huge bottle of wine out of a carrier bag and proceeded to open it just by pressing the cork in with his thumb, and to drink greedily from it. We sat side by side. I was numb and confused, trying hard to make sense of the discrepancy between those adjacent situations either side of the church door. I felt help-less, powerless and hopeless. Christ lives in him too. How can I see God in this man? Even more unlikely it felt to me, how can he possibly see Christ in me? That order of service was headed, Highest in all creation, he lives among the least. He journeys with the rejected and welcomes the weary. And then the invitation, "Come now all who seek and be warmed by the fire of love".

Are strangers so warmed by us? How can we allow ourselves to be inspired afresh to look how our spiritual communities, our churches, can be more effective in celebrating each other's differences rather than being afraid of them? Because we are often afraid or suspicious of the different, aren't we? But it is appropriate to remember that though each of us feels like the 'norm', we are actually the 'different' to others. In some recent research young people voiced that they found it difficult to relate to the people they see running the C of E, describing them as 'White haired men with dodgy dress sense'.

I had to go into a betting shop once on a 'pastoral' visit. I remember the trepidation I felt on crossing the threshold to somewhere so unfamiliar; somewhere where I wasn't sure I would know how to behave appropriately. Thresh-

75

olds can be places of transformation, crossing places. I have come to so appreciate how the URC church I attend now, Zion, offers a 'threshold' to many different contexts and I pay tribute to that.

'Come now, all who seek and be warmed by the fire of love.'

**

And now a young boy joins me as we both set off in our warming cloaks…

****

Harry and the Cloak
Matthew 25: 35

It is the week, not the night before Christmas. It is freezing cold and the sky looms grey, heavy and menacing over Brafferton and Helperby. My heart sank...but it had to be done!

Two small boys lay snuggled in their beds on a Grandma and Grandad visit – the very first without their parents. I entered their room and asked if either of them would like to come with me on a special morning which happened once a year, to take gifts to the elderly people in the villages. Heads burrowed deeper, then one popped out and said, "Yes, if I'm allowed to sing them my special carol from school; and if I can wear my king's crown and cloak from Mrs East's Nativity as a sort of practice".

I explained to little Harry that we would take my shopping basket, with several bags, one for each road in our villages. In these bags would be little brown envelopes with money inside; a small gift for each elderly person, from the church and a village fund of ancient foundation. (The criteria for such designation still remains a mystery to me, however, but I always did and still do trust this particular 'chancellor of the exchequer'.) Off we set down the hill, Harry in my wake, both in our cloaks! The snow began to fall.

That morning we called in many homes of my friends and neighbours – who all knew this gift would be coming – but the joy of Harry coming as well was a total and obviously welcome surprise to them! Thus, the job took longer than usual this particular year as we were inevitably invited in, beginning with Nancy at the back of her old shop. Into that small room we went around the coal fire and clothes horse airer, where Harry handed over her small brown envelope and sure enough told her he wanted to sing to her. Her face lit up and she listened entranced! Harry took his stance in his crown and cloak, (normally a shy child, let's not forget); hands on hips, one leg bent at knee behind and one foot forward on the other leg pumping up and down in time and rhythm to the Twelve Days of Christmas. This was repeated in so many homes that Christmas and gave great giggling joy to these people. I'm not sure they heard all the words as they were not the ones you may know, (not rude or blasphemous you will be pleased to hear!) but it didn't seem to make any difference.

With our basket emptied of coins, bags and envelopes we struggled home through the now 'deep and crisp and even' snow. So, did we arrive home with an empty basket? No. Harry and I realised that there was more in it than when we had left home, several hours earlier. He had given such pleasure to these people, taking their gifts and singing to them, that he returned bearing gifts to himself from them! He was laden down with oranges, satsumas, a selection box, chocolate tree decorations, sweets, an angel and even one or two 50ps.

At one of the Christmas services, one of the young Mums said, "I saw you and Harry in your cloaks last week, walking down Main Street to take the envelopes as the snow began to fall. As I was trudging a few paces behind, the pair of you looked like King Wenceslas and his page!"...

Therefore, Christian folk be sure, wealth or rank possessing,
Ye who now will bless the poor shall yourselves find blessing!

**

Finally, reflecting on my baby and small child decade…

****

The Midwife
Luke 2: 1-20, Matthew2: 11

I am exhausted. My husband and I keep one of the busiest inns in Bethlehem; life is hectic, even in normal times, let alone at this census time. People are pouring into the town and not moving on. Hospitality is my 'thing' and I hate to turn anyone away. At this time we are absolutely packing them in, doubling up on rooms, some sleeping in corridors, as people are desperate for shelter. And the food…slaughtering, grinding, brewing, boiling, cooking, baking, serving, heating water and washing up! My feet are killing me and the sweat is pouring off me as I rush hither and thither.

There is another knock and my husband shuffles reluctantly to open the door as it is impossible to allow in another single guest. His heart sinks as he sees before him a young couple completely exhausted and the young woman obviously in the late stages of pregnancy. 'No. I am sorry ', he gestures, lifting his shoulders helplessly, thinking also, 'I am not sure we want trouble like this anyway!'

I peer out from behind him and look into their faces, tired, hungry, anxious, gentle and hopeful. They tentatively say that they know this is the place for them to be, anywhere will do, and so I hesitatingly suggest to Reuben that we do have the animal shed at the back which at least is warm, dry and we could provide lanterns. My sixth sense told me that it was important to help them if we possibly could, whilst my heart sank as I saw her belly! Her hand rests on the mound of her baby safe for now inside, but not for much longer by the look of her.

Reuben took them round the back and gave them some rough bedding which was all we had left. The soft steamy breath of the few animals we had warmed the stable and he left the couple settled in the straw alongside the manager, with a lantern hung from the rafters, and he said I would be back shortly with some water for cleansing after their long journey.

Well, it was a while before I could get back, and by then it was late evening, yet a particularly bright star was in the sky that night lighting the way. I certainly needed the water because when I returned I was greeted by a groaning. I lifted the latch and entered. The smells, mingling in with the smell of breath and straw in that space, had changed; there was activity; I felt the anxiety and I saw by the light of the lantern, that the young woman was in labour, her husband looking terrified. The smell was the smell of birth fluids and it seemed that time stood still; suspended. I put down my bowl and moved gently to help her. I had done this before for other women although I had no children myself. Locals said that I had a gift for it. I had a certain stillness in the waiting, encouraging, supporting and the skill of safely delivering new life into the world. Forgetting all my other responsibilities, I stayed alongside now, kneeling in the straw, working and reassuring until with a final groan from the mother the baby boy slipped into my hands, clothed only in blood and fluid, perfect and alive, a new creation! I wrapped him in the old towel I had brought with me and passed him into his mother's arms, helping him to fix onto the nipple of her soft, rounded abreast, and his hungry little mouth pulled and sucked and tasted. The mother felt the tug which sent a current through her body. The young father stood alongside and knew, and although he did not know quite what it was that he knew, he did know. She looked at me deeply, our eyes meeting as she thanked me.

Later I returned to take bread and wine which was all I had left after feeding so many. I could hardly believe my eyes, the place was full of men! Shepherds by the look of them, as one of them had a new born lamb. What on earth or in Heaven's name is going on here? I thought the smells were very different now! They said they had come because they had heard singing on the hillside that night which could even have been angels, telling them to come, and come they had, running.

The father knew...I knew although I did not know what I knew. The shepherds knew too, although they weren't sure what it was they knew, although they did know about new born lambs, gift, a delivery born to deliver, and sacrifice!

I had gazed, I had heard, I had touched, I had smelt, and I had tasted, and in my sixth sense I had experienced awe and wonder of such magnitude, that it bewildered and shook me.

I resolved to keep an eye on them until they moved on. They were in one way just some of my many guests at that time, but life was different after that. You might think when you are as old, as wise and as experienced in life as I am, nothing much can surprise you, but that night, in the straw, in the lantern light, helped by a very bright star piercing through the gaps in the planks, I had experienced in all my sense what it was to be present at a unique delivery, brought to birth, like and yet unlike any other, a new creation.

After a week or so, they were ready to consider moving on, the mother was getting stronger, so I went across one day to say 'goodbye' to them, but that day I could not get to cross the yard. Such a commotion and carrying on was going on for most of the day. There were camels and three very grand gentlemen and a lot of excitement as people were curious to see them, being so rich looking and different from us. The camels were dressed up as well as the men! Lost their way, obviously!

So next day I went over again to see this new little family, but the stable was empty of all but the animals, flattened straw and the manger bathed in a shaft of golden sunlight. It looked as if they had left in a hurry, the baby's wrapping clothes lying in a body shape in a dark corner, but again a distinctive smell; this time fragrance of myrrh or frankincense, or even both.

A mystery...yet of course I wasn't too sure what the mystery was that I understood without understanding. But that is the true mystery, isn't it?

**

But Mary did know and pondered all these things in her heart, as she gave birth that night to the Lord of all Creation; and fed the one who would grow up to offer food to the whole world…himself the bread which he brought.

******

A nativity scene in St Mary, Myton Church

Chapter 4

And then the feminist woman (what, no bra?), full of strange and new experiences; lifestyle challenged, sudden and quick in energy; spontaneous in decision for better or worse!

All Zipped up
and Out
I Go

1981-1995

In which I made more than a few mistakes...returned to work outside the home...Emma was diagnosed with Acute Lymphoblastic Leukaemia with feared only a week to live.

The Fourth Age

Naked and you clothed me
i)   Hockliffe House
ii)   Brave New World
iii)   Returning to Work outside the Home
iv)   Spangly Toes on Leaving ITU
v)   My Precious Anna Cross
vi)   Between Angels and Demons
vii)   Glory in the Gloom
viii)   The Gorgeous Nightie in the Oncology Ward
ix)   Hannah's PCSO Uniform

Naked and you called me
x)   The Red Shoes. Important for Adventure, but best not to leave them on too long!
xi)   Glory or Rags. Mary Magdalen who has recently been made an 'Apostle' by Pope Francis! Should she be Red or Blue?
xii)   Another Trinity?

Naked and you clothed me

Hockliffe House

Finally, the Old Shoe in North Buckinghamshire burst at the seams. Paul had his own bookshop in Dunstable, so we moved over the county boundary into Bedfordshire to be nearer, into a completely unexpected situation. It was a large Georgian farmhouse, with medieval origins of a St John's Hospital, Hockliffe House. It had a well in the cellar, a butler's pantry, a dairy, a huge kitchen with an Aga and a bread oven, a dining hall, a drawing room, a sitting room, a library, eight bedrooms and a bathroom with two doors which had been created on what was really a landing, so there was much passing through in every sense! It had a glorious coffin sized Art Deco bath and a loose plastic-tiled ceiling which blew off every time the wind was a bit gusty, exposing the rafters. We could afford it because it was smack on the A5 with traffic roaring right outside the drawing room. The grounds were about 1½ acres, comprising dilapidated vine house with its own still thriving vine and defunct boiler house, a sunken garden, a herb garden, glorious ancient yew hedges, an orchard, a huge weeping ash and an empty circular pond which we renovated complete with naked statue. A little woodland ran alongside one boundary and the rest was flanked by a red brick wall. This is where we brought up our family for about 25 years. When we came to sell it, I wrote an enticing advertisement, thus:

A rare opportunity to acquire this historic well-loved family home and place of hospitality for centuries.

Unashamedly 'shabby-chic', this large house, combining Georgian elegance with unpretentious, generous accommodation, is perfect for today's family life.

York flagged hall and quarry tiled passages…for toddlers on tricycles.

Many rooms, cupboards, hidey-holes…for hide and seek.

To accommodate growing families, eight large bedrooms…for 'own space', or lots of sleepovers!

Quiet rooms, noisy rooms, secluded rooms up a private staircase…for teenagers. It has an adjoining convenient drainpipe up to these quarters for aspiring Romeos.

Legendary for parties, soirées and hospitality, dating back to medieval times: yet private and uniquely distinctive for those today who like something 'apart'.

The warm heart of this house is the huge, oak beamed farmhouse kitchen, where family and friends gather around the red Aga situated alongside an ancient bread oven.

It has a large walled 'secret garden', where children can play with freedom. Those seeking peace and quiet can sit in shady wooded areas, sunken garden, or around the naked lady pond and fountain, York flagged yard and barbecue area.

Jeremy (standing)
William and Ann (seated)
Tim. Hannah. Emma (front. left to right)

This is an unusual property, and not one for the faint-hearted, but it has a magic of its own, with its unique sense of history, peace, seclusion and solitude, despite being situated on a busy main road. In fact, on this ancient Roman highway, this property can be recognized by the discerning as ideally placed for commuters, with nearby access for motorway, railway stations and airport.

**

It was to form the backdrop to a major section of my Christian life and calling, a privilege in so many ways as 'caretakers' there for our allotted span...

******

Brave New World

An elderly Deaconess friend of mine, instead of a 40th birthday card, sent me a plaque which read:
'Everything up to the age of 40 is just a rehearsal'.

It seemed amusing at the time, but a bit strange. Well, I had had all these children, had been married for 20 years, done a degree at home, what is all this a rehearsal for? Eventually, however, I came to recognise its wisdom and probably made more serious mistakes during this phase of my life than at any other time - well, thus far anyway! And an imminent serious medical crisis for my elder daughter shattered the previous equilibrium. After all those years at home as a full-time mother and housewife, suddenly I turned a corner for which I was largely unprepared. Here came a transition time from what had gone before and of which I was still a part, to an exploration of who I was to become in the wider world. The discovery was in parts alarming, exciting, dangerous and dazzling. In retrospect, this period of my life was possibly even more treacherous than those tumultuous years of my adolescence had been.

I tentatively navigated my way through, beginning to grow and flourish aesthetically in my church Reader ministry, in its choir, plus spending some of most weekends in Oxford as a mother of New College and Christ Church Cathedral Choir choristers. My relationship network exploded quickly; building on the foundation of my Arts degree I continued to grow in reading, art appreciation, participation in music, attending concerts and particularly losing myself in the college choral Evensongs. As I returned to work - Housing Benefits and then Hospital Chaplaincy - I had money for the first and only time in my life, so could buy clothes, and go and choose them. In Oxford I rejoiced in the glorious hippie bazaar type of garments, impregnated with that unmistakeable fragrance of patchouli. More of my Chaplaincy clothes later, but for Housing Benefits in Dunstable I wore the smartest and most feminine that Next could offer. To my slight surprise I loved working there and even learned to use computers, which has stood me in good stead ever since.

**

So how did I come to work there?...

But first, Kirsty Wark on Clothing and Feminism:
Guardian Magazine
The broadcaster's thoughts are evidence, contrary to what sometimes seems popular belief, that feminism and interest in clothing can co-exist, 'Why should it be antithetical to feminism to be interested in style, in design, in line and colour and cut? Why would a desire to feel good about yourself be at odds with feminism?... Surely feminism should allow women to be as complicated and contradictory in their personalities as we allow men to be, with their football teams and fishing rods!'

******

85

Returning to Work outside the Home

By this time, I felt rich in life experience. 'Back in the day' in the Sixties I was offered every job I applied and was interviewed for. These varied from ECG work, library, laboratory technician, administration, and others, as we moved around whilst Paul was establishing his career as a bookseller and publisher. I had dipped my toe into the world of work outside the home as a part-time sales rep for his infant local publishing enterprise which complemented the bookshop he had opened in Dunstable. But the search for full time employment was now very different. Every door on which I knocked was closed to me. For some I had had no experience with computers, and technology had raced ahead whilst I was at home full time. As I applied for increasingly menial work, I was then told 'You are overqualified'. Finally, after one such reaction at my interview for a Clerical Assistant post, I went back to the Personnel Department with this conundrum. A response!

It was at the time of the unpopular Community Charge tax and a period of great angst and anguish, especially amongst the people who were in receipt of benefit. Angry scenes were commonplace in the reception area of the council offices and their usual young girl clerical assistants were struggling to cope. So I was offered this role as an older and more experienced person, with the promise of a review of status anon, and so subsequently, zipped up, out I went, moving on after two or three years to my Hospital Chaplaincy - where clothing became an interesting issue as I wandered around the wards.

Because I was a lay minister (Reader), I wore no dog collar, so others, especially clergy, used to ask, 'Don't you find this a disadvantage as people will not know who you are?' Well, they did have a point and it did depend on what I wore as to how I was initially 'recognised'. In a smart suit it was thought I was a social worker; a soft floaty dress in summer once, a ballet dancer; in my black mini skirt, even a hairdresser; and if I wore my Celtic cross, yes, the chaplain. However, these 'disguises' did mean that patients did not feel they had to pretend to be asleep as I approached their bedside! Also, to have assumed that I was in another role entirely did open the way for conversation and an exchange which frequently did drift to Godly conversation. I was privileged to share many life stories in that place. That work was a difficult and humbling and precious experience and one where I learned that the other staff you needed to know and work most closely with were the porters and the switchboard ladies!

I cannot leave this without mentioning that guesswork happened the other way round too. Very occasionally a patient did actually request a chaplaincy visit and I really did begin to recognise ladies in their beds as I approached as to what their Christian denomination might be. Sweet little ladies with smiley faces, snugly relaxed in their beds, were usually Roman Catholics. I learned so much from them and their steadfast and certain faith. Anglicans presented in smart bed gear and usually sitting upright with their hair 'set', whilst Methodists could be recognised by their stiff handbags with upstanding sticky-up handles, perched on the locker. May I be forgiven?! Incidentally these handbags are currently in great demand in charity shops, now being described as 'Vintage'!

**

But this was serious work too and in retrospect one for which my theological Reader training had in no way prepared me; and with those words we move to the patient who was just moving on from ITU...

******

Spangly Toes on Leaving ITU
Written in 2015

This nail varnish saved my life, giving me a will to live, which is why I keep it with me always to remember and be thankful. I was the senior night sister in the local hospital and I have not, nor ever have had, any formal faith, but we are here tonight to talk not about religion, but about spiritual needs and, Oh boy, did I have those!
Unexpected introductory words, as you will see.
I was standing at the front of a group one evening, in about 2000, as the guest speaker for about twenty volunteers who were training to be Hospice at Home visitors. On this evening for considering the spiritual needs of the terminally ill and their carer, I was there because I had been a hospital chaplain for four years in a large general hospital, designated as a major crisis unit, which was encircled by four potential major accident danger zones - main line railway, the M1, football ground and airport. I write this today having heard on the local radio that hospital chaplains may be expendable in an era soon predicted when only a small minority of patients have any formal faith at all. The appalling shortsightedness of this tragedy is that everyone has a spirit, which at these times can be frequently in as much distress as anything physical or mental about their whole selves.
As I was about to start, a lady in her forties held up her hand and asked if she could address the gathering before I spoke. She reached into her handbag and produced a bottle of bright red nail varnish which she held up for all to see. This was her story which I have permission to share here.
I had had what was considered to be a fatal car accident in Spain and was flown back home to die. I was unconscious for several weeks with very severe head and face damage and many of the bones in my body broken. Eventually I began to emerge from the darkness and yet in some way was in a merciful land of not-knowing, and was lying on a mattress on a side ward floor, pretty well naked, thrashing about in confusion and anger. I was secured, trapped and surrounded by traction and lay helpless, in agony of body, mind and spirit. I saw the hospital chaplain come in - called for as no one else knew what to do with me. That was Ann, who is here tonight. I swore very badly at her and asked, 'What the f... is a chaplain here for, GET OUT.' But Ann stayed, sat alongside,

87

listened and took all the abuse and then asked, 'Is there anything at all I could do for you?' 'No,' I replied. 'All I want is to paint my f'ing toe nails and you're not b'... going to do that for me, are you?'

And Ann found the bright red nail varnish in my locker, and that is what she did. I lay from then on gazing down through all the terrible stuff going on around me and would stare at my twinkly, sparkly red toe nails and knew they were a sign that I could get well, be pretty and myself again.

I didn't really have to explain after that what the spiritual needs of the critically ill might be.

**

I mentioned earlier about the Celtic Cross I used to wear in that place, a simple silver cross surrounded by the Celtic circle. Here follows a story of another very unusual and precious jewellery cross which I received recently from my friend Anna...

******

My Precious Anna Cross
Written in 2015

Anna is my dear friend and Open University Tutor of many years ago. Paula Mather was her godmother, once a student at the Boston School of Arts and Crafts, 1924-1926. Paula crafted the cross as her goldsmith piece for that course. The family had arrived in Boston from Lundholm, Sweden. The father of this family was a doctor, bringing with him four children; Arthur, Edward, Ruth and Dagma. Dagma was Anna's mother. Ruth was a nurse at Boston Mass and Paula, her daughter. Anna's paternal grandmother was a Quaker.

Paula had a passionate Christian faith, which is why Anna has entrusted me with the cross. She was engaged to a fiancé whom she deeply loved. During the Depression of 1929 he went away to do field work and died. Paula never recovered fully. She worked as a social secretary to a Mrs Lyman, whom she accompanied all round the world. (Anna added in order to help me understand an American perspective on this role, 'This Mrs Lyman would have been equivalent in standing to Mrs Rockefeller.')

The cross is described, for insurance purposes, as: Ornate, eighteen carat, yellow gold, cultured pearl and emerald cross. Twelve grain-set, cultured half pearls with four princess-cut box set emeralds surrounding the centre of the cross. Emeralds weigh approximately .30 ct each. (1.20 ct in total). Value 29.9.11 £1,550.

I intend to bequeath it to Hannah.

With the cross was a large emerald-coloured stone which I have had set into a single earring. It is paste but is thought to have been a copy of a very valuable original, probably held in a safe by Paula. She was a very wealthy woman and such a copy would probably have been made as a safe way to protect the genuine original from theft whilst the wearer was out and about! So, if people ask me when I wear this earring, 'Is it a genuine emerald?' I respond, with a twinkle in the eye, 'No, just a copy. The real one is in the safe at home! '

**

To Anna I owe a great deal in terms of fun, companionship and learning. She has helped me through the terrible experience of Emma's brush with death and its aftermath ever since...

******

Between Angels and Demons
Written in 2005

There was a time about 15 years ago when I remember being a normal-ish Mum, with five normal-ish teenage children. The day after, I walked on wobbly legs out of a hospital, got into my 2CV with one of my young sons, and by some miracle drove to Oxford where he was a chorister; I think I remember collapsing in New College Chapel that night after a ridiculous thought, 'How can they all be there singing Byrd Responses, when I have a handbag full of books on Leukaemia, and Emma will probably die before the end of the week?'

And that was just the beginning. As we sought as a family to find our way through the experience of our daughter's late diagnosis of an aggressive cancer, I recall feeling that I was lost in an alien landscape without a map. We were told the day after Emma's diagnosis that siblings often became very disturbed, even sometimes taking to criminal pursuits; also, alarmingly, that up to 90% of leukaemic children's parents' marriages end in divorce.

Against the odds as a family we have survived intact; but not without a legacy of much grief, pain, learning from our mistakes, black humour, and living with the underacknowledged financial implications of long term illness. Emma's sister spoke recently of having for years believed that everyone would rather it had been her than Emma, but, of course, at thirteen years old she could never have articulated that. We now know also that she only learned of Emma's illness by overhearing our telephone conversations about it with others. How can this have been? We felt all along that we had kept all the children informed as best we could in the shock and grief of it all. We hadn't. I heard it suggested that if a teenage boy has a mother or older sister whose life is terminally threatened, he may find it difficult subsequently to make long term relationships with women for fear of them leaving him. When I gently broached this eventually with Jeremy, our eldest, then about 24 years old, he wept. On one occasion at nine years old, our youngest son, William, out with Emma in Oxford, had to stand by helplessly, whilst others looked on in fear, as she had a violent steroid psychotic fit in the bus station; he picked up her college bag and quietly took her home. Tim, our middle son, has never been able to really talk about it at all.

Emma's book about that first traumatic year of her illness, Between Angels and Demons, has prompted me to reflect that some of my worst fears for her have been realised. Her endocrine system has been destroyed. The cranial radiotherapy has caused degenerative effects on all her organs, her immune system is shot to pieces. Her eyesight is fast deteriorating, she has had surgery for skin cancers on her beautiful face, her thyroid is damaged and she cannot eat a meal or even have a drink without becoming unconscious afterwards for over an hour. As a result of that long ago steroid treatment and too rapid withdrawal, she continues to have psychotic fits if her brain is startled by something as simple as a book falling from a table. She has an allergy to petrol-based chemicals so is now confined to her home in the forest, and can no longer travel safely.

Reaching for the stars

Somehow despite all her suffering, Emma remains stunning and vibrant. Even during her early treatment, she arrived at Oxford to take a degree in English where she met her future husband, Lorenzo. He had been told that a very sick girl was arriving; then when she did, he describes her as having a 'life force, with a mind alight with eager curiosity', and wanting to marry her from that moment. They are still, 12 years on, deeply in love and enjoy life hugely as far as they are able. People stood at the book launch and wept as they gave her a standing ovation. One lady said that from now on, in their house, there would be an 'Emma Box,' where everyone would have to put in a pound every time they whinged! This would be sent to the Teenage Cancer Trust. Between Angels and Demons would make you laugh and would make you cry. It is written with energy, courage, humour and trust in a God who Emma knows has sustained her through it all.

N.B. A fuller version of this article was published in Home and Family, the journal publication of the Mother's Union. 2005

Afterword

Thousands of people for over 25 years now have prayed for the healing of the critical situation Emma's body has been left in after the too harsh, ravaging treatment, which has kept her alive but left her severely disabled for life as the rest of us know it. Prayer and how, or even if, it is answered remains a mystery, but we know that it matters. I read once these words which I have never forgotten whilst I am on occasion ruminating and questioning the efficacy of intercessory prayer:

Prayer does not change God, but it always changes him who prays.
Soren Kierkegaard

**

Now read how Emma experienced the transforming nature of clothes even in adversity...

******

Glory in the Gloom
Written in 2013

Emma writes:

Even in the depths of the direst moments of my illness I felt the power of clothes to 'transform', not just visually but inside too. I remember Mummy's clothes being significant to me at this time as she sat alongside me, in her blue velvet skinny top and long blue flowing skirt. Together with her hair and eyes it conveyed an overall sense and glory of blue and gold that accompanies her to this day no matter what she is wearing. One day she brought me a nightie.

The moment that I slipped the glorious, slinky, ivory-satin sheath over my head I was no longer a patient with just days to live but a 1940s film star - just as you in knowing me so well had foreseen! In that instant - and in your immense love - you gave me a way to hold on to my femininity despite the loss of my hair and curves. And crucially too, the gowns - and they were definitely more 'gowns' than 'nighties'! In their catalogue, I remember, Next was showcasing them in a ballroom, as though they were evening gowns, to highlight their glamour! A nightdress inexorably helped distance me from the other-worldly horrors that threatened to overwhelm me night and day as I fought to hold on to living. They did not belong to this nightmare realm. And neither did I!

91

Of course, once the dastardly Demons saw the combination of exquis-ite little satin slippers and matching dressing gown they knew they didn't stand a chance!

And the 'transformative' power of clothes is really at the heart of what makes this subject so fascinating, isn't it? A piece of cloth can be distinctive or beautiful but cut and fashion it into a garment - or even simply define it as a shawl - and it can conjure all kinds of magic! Which made me think of Mr Benn*, and of how brilliantly he exemplifies this idea! Into the changing room he steps, discarding his work-a-day 'uniform' of pin stripes and bowler hat, and as if by magic - 'which of course it was!' - he can become whoever he dreams of being, simply by changing his attire! (Do you think that could explain that phase when I was about 13/14 and changing my outfit four or five times a day? Perhaps I was actually simply trying to find my identity!)

*Mr Benn is a children's book and T.V. character.

**

And now Emma offers a story of just one of the adventures of the nightie...

******

92

The Gorgeous Nightie in the Oncology Ward
Written in 2014

Emma writes:

There is an incident involving the beautiful nightdress that illustrates so movingly the way that clothing can have a significance in our lives more profound than the practical purposes of keeping us warm, preserving our modesty or indicating position, rank or denomination.

It was the morning after that dreadful night when you had to race me back into the hospital with a life-threatening fever and then were forced to leave me by the officious night nurse. Miraculously God had carried me through hell again and out the other side. I climbed Bambi-legged out of bed and made my way through the ward full of elderly, dying people to the bathroom. On my return the old lady in the bed opposite beckoned me over to her side. With eyes shining with tears she took my hand. She told me that during the night she had finally given up the will to live and had resolved not to fight any longer. And then she had seen me gliding past the end of her bed in my ethereal shimmering gown like a beautiful ballerina and she knew that God had sent one of his Angels down from Heaven to tell her that He was with her and to give her the strength to carry on. She said that when her family came to see her that day she would have a smile for them for the first time in as long as they would remember...

And God and that beautiful nightdress made two miracles in one that morning as that lady's beautiful words, her faith and my new-found sense that even in my own vulnerability and the nightmare realm which I now inhabited I could still reach out and touch the lives of others - perhaps even help them - gave me renewed courage and heart and the determination to do so for as long as He kept me alive and dancing!

And then there you were again at the end of the ward with your love and smile and my freshly washed, spare, miracle nightdress and I knew that all really was right with the world once more and somehow would always be so...!

**

And many years later my other lovely daughter also had a humbling experience of how her attire had a defining and transformative effect. It is not surprising after all that she had experienced in our family life that her real ambition had been to be a firefighter! However, truth and inspiration need know no boundaries. She has always been a bonus to any situation...

******

93

Hannah's PCSO Uniform
Written in 2015

Woman's Hour. We are what we wear
Question to PC Ellie Bloggs:
    How do you do style with a police uniform? How are you judged?
Reply:
    You don't have to think what you wear as you get dressed. A Police uniform brings legal power. It is iconic. In the mirror, you can see 'you' in it. People have an emotional reaction to you. Even when you are not wearing it, you can have the authority it has given you by mistake.
    Ellie gave an example of authority in the wrong context, likening it to the insight that she had 'become' the uniform, like Dorothy and the Red Shoes!

My younger daughter reflects:
    I had reached the age of 34 and my two beautiful boys were both in full-time education and it was now time for me to decide in which direction my career was heading. I had continued to work throughout the boys' baby and toddler years but felt now I had been presented with an opportunity for change. Not to work was an option I couldn't explore both for financial and for self-preservation reasons (!), so what was I to do next?
    Returning to a desk job in market research was a daunting prospect, so I became determined to embrace a new career of my choosing. A lifelong dream to become a firefighter appeared to be well out of reach, so I turned instead to the police force. Here I was fortunate enough to pass numerous qualification stages, and even surprisingly my fitness test, to become a full-time Police Community Support Office (PCSO).
    Even now, six years later, I remember the pride I felt at my induction ceremony; I had done it! As the eldest member of our training intake (by some way), I had become the mother figure to my training colleagues and my pride extended to them too. As we stood, lined up in our smartly pressed uniforms, we were announcing our joining of an institution, willing and now qualified to protect and serve the public. Our specific roles in the force were very clear and whilst not 'actual' police officers, we were proud to 'belong'. This of course was the first role of our uniform; our sense of 'belonging' and commitment would be made clear to the public and all those whom we encountered.
    Four pieces of clothing, consisting of black itchy trousers, blue T-shirt, hat and a fluorescent yellow stab-vest, gave us a new and clear identity. In training it was made clear that wearing our uniforms came with great responsibility. Our actions would be highly scrutinized and judged by people, not only because of the uniform but for what we represented whilst wearing it. Contrary to an originally naive perspective, this uniform transpired not always to be an item in my favour and in fact, would often be to my detriment! I swiftly realised that encountering me in uniform posed different ideologies to different people, not always representing the positive image that I'd hoped or believed it would.

To offer some perspective on this, after induction I was placed within a community policing team in a rather challenging area of a large town. A six month ban on PCSOs patrolling in the area without a police officer (for personal safety) had just been lifted. We were now tasked with re-engaging with the community, attempting to re-build the trust and cohesive partnership lost between ourselves and our immediate public. Emotions were high and I set out on day one, in my uniform, with the inevitable realization that I was about to spectacularly sink or swim!

Fortunately, I'm pleased to report I believe I managed to swim! However, an initial realization highlighted how stereotypes and pre-conceived judgments had constructed an obscure and warped perspective of one another, and this was a challenge I had to overcome. My uniform and who I represented meant I would have to work hard to be accepted by my community and I had my own prejudices to conquer also. Somehow, I knew a need to ensure my genuine desire to 'belong' to their community too shone past my external appearance. Reassurances must be offered that I could actually remain in both 'camps'. So, rightly or wrongly I had to earn this sense of 'belonging' and respect by ensuring my personality and hard work became more prevalent than my uniform.

I genuinely believe this was easier being a female and the public often visibly received me more favourably than my male colleagues. I'm not sure if my feminine side initially seemed less threatening but I certainly encountered less resistance when arriving at jobs. Obviously in heightened or aggressive situations the presence of a male officer was always reassuring, both for us and the public alike, but often a female presence appeared to naturally defuse situations. On reflection, this was possibly out of a conscious or un-conscious respect for a 'bird' (as I was often referred to) being present! Or, based on many innuendos proposed to me by men whilst on patrol, a female in 'uniform' presented another perception to them of a possibly more recreational basis! Although, as my husband often reminded me, the reality of my uniform was far from the image often portrayed and PCSOs certainly did not have handcuffs!

My uniform was also often a topic of conversation for children (challenging or otherwise) and interestingly it meant they were always keen to talk to me whilst I was out and about. I remember one young girl being astounded that at the end of my shift I went home and changed into clothes just like her. She said, 'I thought you wore that 'suit' all the time. Does that mean you're like me then really?' I replied that I was absolutely just like her.

Simplistically, this little girl had highlighted that once in uniform (for whatever reason) we are seen as setting ourselves apart from the rest. A uniform seems to provide an assumed identity and an immediate sense of 'belonging' to a group of people. It appears to allow others the 'right' to assume either a positive or negative judgment about who you are, your status in society maybe and even your beliefs or principles. A uniform shouldn't mean you lose your individuality or 'define' you, but maybe the very nature of it does impinge on this, either ever so slightly or significantly, if we and society allow us to do so.

I always remained incredibly proud to wear my uniform. It provided many benefits (aside from protection) and automatically allowed me a privileged access into people's life and homes. However, I hope my uniform did not ever 'define' who I was. I believe that even those people, who did not whole-heartily approve of the institution I represented, still learned to accept and even like me! Gratefully, they were able to see past my fluorescent jacket and trust that I was actually just a person the same as them, simply trying to fulfil my commitment to serve and protect. In turn, I also learned not to make swift judgments about others and to look past exteriors or the prejudices society has placed on appearance and what we wear. Our uniforms can say so much about us but let's not also forget what's underneath.

**

She loves pretty shoes too, as do I, especially the odd and unusual ones…

…*give a girl the right shoes and she can conquer the world.* Marilyn Monroe

******

Naked and you called me

The Red Shoes

I have been known to have an eccentric taste in shoes, especially my red ones. They were fun to wear, but a bit challenging to the institution when worn under my robes. I celebrated the current pope making them respectable! There is a well-known traditional story about red shoes. It is about a poor little beggar girl who longed to dance in sparkly shiny shoes; but she made the mistake of giving up her shabby handcrafted ones and accepting a pair of new red ones from the seductive lady in the golden coach. And indeed she danced, and danced and danced, until in the end she couldn't get them off, and the grisly ending does not bear thinking about here! How on earth might a pair of red shoes help us to explore an aspect of the call to waiting and stillness of the Advent period, that waiting time or preparation weeks running up to Christmas?

Food and Raiment
2 Thess 3: 6-13

This reading in Thessalonians raises many Christian instructions which may make us feel uncomfortable today. It might speak to us as the 'stir-up' and 'wake up' call as Advent approaches. That time when we prepare our hearts, not only to celebrate the birth of Jesus, but also His second coming. Here is a challenge as a time of accountability for us all.

For we hear that some of you are living in idleness; mere busy bodies. Not doing any work! An ambiguous phrase, 'Busy bodies, yet not doing any work'. Surely if we are busy, it means we are doing a lot of work. Or does it?

Perhaps what we are so busy doing is not always the most effective work for the furthering of the Kingdom and our own souls. Perhaps that is what Paul means here. Most of us know, don't we, the Protestant work ethic? That which drives us on to keep pushing ourselves - feeling guilty if we stop. We must rush off to this meeting, that group, even when we're tired. If there is anything which gets pushed aside in our day, it will very possibly be our time for being still and quietly waiting on God. Allowing him to be busy with us, instead of always feeling we have to be busy for him.

I remember reading an article once, 'Are you a human being or an inhuman being?' As human beings, our frames are not meant for perpetual motion, yet that is what most of us subject ourselves to. Always just one more goal to be accomplished. Where is the boundary which says 'Stop! I have done enough for today? I owe it to myself, as well as to God, to take time to be still, in body, mind and spirit.'

'Mere busy bodies, not doing any work.'

Well, Advent is the waiting time. Are we going to be so busy that the real work of Advent is not done? Are we going to be such busy bodies and so exhausted that we miss him when he comes?

One of the things which we might lose in our busy lives is the art of storytelling; the passing down from one generation to another of stories of eternal wisdom and truth. Jesus did that all the time. Taking everyday incidents to weave stories around, to teach the people of those days about where God is in day to day living. And they are as powerful today. But there are other ancient tales of myth, legend and folk lore which also speak of profound yet simple wisdom. One of the riches of our culture is these stories and there is a real danger that they will be lost in the wilderness of a culture where TV and videos rule. One of the greatest gifts that parents can pass on to their children is the wisdom of these stories whilst sitting reading alongside them. Like the parables, once you've heard them you remember them forever.

...not 'made for walking'

Remembering the sorry tale of Red Shoes, we are reminded, especially as women, about the importance of our equipment and clothing for healthy adventure, courage, risk and danger. But the warning is that eventually we may not be still enough to stop 'dancing' at all, if we let those shoes take control of us. The shoes took control of that little girl in the fairy tale.

Do we ever learn? At the end of a certain week, after working three seventeen-hour days on the run, I was advised to cancel my afternoon engagements by a trusted friend, and stop! 'No,' I said, 'I can't possibly. I have to do this, this and this. I can't let people down.' 'Can you move things to another time?' she asked. 'No,' I replied. Then I realised. I just did not know how to stop. Dance, dance, dance, until we drop exhausted.

Do you recognise it in your own life!? 'Mere busy-bodies'. I began to realise that I was almost at the stage when I did not even know how to get the red shoes off. So, I did before it was too late, at great cost to my ego (so hard to know we're not indispensable, isn't it?) but probably at very little cost to those

98

who were quite happy to be flexible. A busy body. Thank God for those who care about us enough to point out the wisdom of the Red Shoes. As the Jews reach the Sabbath, they stop as if their work is done. So that God can be busy with them.

The final words of that reading are, 'Brothers and sisters, do not tire of doing what is right'. So, what is right or not right in my pattern of living either in Advent or at any other time? What is the balance in my life between work, resting and playing even? Will we be so busy, busy, dancing, dancing to exhaustion, that we miss him when he comes?

So, the darkness shall be the light; and the stillness, the dancing.
T.S. Eliot...*East Coker*

This article first appeared in 'Plus', a quarterly publication by Christians on Aging.

**

More red shoes stories later...but for now a sad reflection on the judgement women receive on attire, even in this case a man 'dressing' a woman in art...

******

Glory or Rags. Mary Magdalen; Should she be Red or Blue?
John 19: 25

In one of the Yorkshire parishes, Thormanby, we decided one year to have a festival to celebrate the patron saint of the little church there. This awesome remote tiny church at the end of a track is of very ancient lineage, even bearing a green man sculpture in the vestry, suggesting pagan provenance of the site. It is legendary that monks from Rievaulx Abbey used this place as their retreat centre before the Dissolution of the Monasteries.

Brian and Heather, gifted and dynamic members of the congregation there at the time, were inspired through their love of art to initiate and create such a festival. Heather writing a report after the event for the Bishops Diocesan book about innovative ways of being church in North Yorkshire urges the less adventurous:

Try something different – try a Patronal Festival

In 2005 we decided to hold a Festival in our tiny 12th Century church over a weekend to celebrate our Patronal Saint, Mary Magdalen. I knew very little, so I set about researching a person who turned out to be something of a feminist icon. My starting point was the Bible and I was amazed to find that Mary Magdalen's reputation as a 'fallen woman' was not based on Biblical texts but on later interpretations eventually brought together by Pope Gregory the Great in AD519. He did this because her status as the first person to see the risen Christ presented a threat to what had become an all-male priesthood.

99

I knew from a visit to The Camargue in Southern France about a legend that Mary Magdalen had sailed to France following the crucifixion. This turned out to be called the Golden Legend and is followed up as the theme of the novel The Da Vinci Code. From visits to Italy I remembered that Mary Magdalen was a popular subject in Renaissance painting and I was able to get pictures of frescoes, stained glass and sculpture as well as panel and oil paintings.

St Mary Magdalen (Donatello) c 1457
Wood, height: 188 cm
Museo dell' Opera del Duomo, Florence

To bring these elements together my husband made four notice boards which were small enough not to dwarf our tiny church but big enough for displays of pictures and information. The biblical references and Pope Gregory's Homily 33 were on the first two boards and the Golden Legend was on the fourth. The third contained a wide variety of interesting and beautiful 'Magdalen' art. The research about the pictures told me that the colours of the women's clothes held a special significance so that Mary Magdalen, the 'sinner', could not be confused with other women, in particular Mary, Mother of Christ. So a group of us put together five themed flower arrangements – white for purity, blue for the colour of heaven, green for the earth, gold for avarice and red for wantonness. We also had a collection of Magdalen symbols and vanities plus a display of books loaned to us by a friendly bookseller. The festival came to an end on

Sunday evening with a Choral Evensong courtesy of a group of singers from another parish which celebrated our Saint in music and prayer.

Subsequent to this article, I have recently discovered that Pope Francis has now officially affirmed Mary Magdalen as an Apostle of Jesus. She was of course the first to see Jesus after his resurrection and was commissioned by him to go and tell all the others, thus the Apostle to the Apostles?

So, to pick up Heather's earlier comment on this saint as a feminist Icon how do you personally feel about the 'Magdalen' art and the interpretation of her clothing over time? The clothing does indeed depict artists are making a judgement on her character. Does this for you reflect on misogynistic understanding of the implied 'fallenness' and defiling nature of women judged on adornment?

**

Happily, in our daily life, we continue to make our own clothing decisions, such that 'clothes allow us to find out who we are', as Thomas Carlyle wrote. 'Know first who you are and then adorn yourself accordingly', Epiclytus advised nearly 2,000 years ago. I am still learning...

******

Another Trinity?
Psalm 45: 13

The King's daughter is all glorious within; her clothing is of wrought gold.

Even whilst I was shopping recently at my favourite greengrocer's shop, a young girl assistant admired my velvet coat. Entering into conversation, I told her I was writing about clothes. Her face lit up in response. "What we wear describes what we are like inside, doesn't it? Not rocket science then.!

I remain astonished that this work began with my father, as he was the adult in my life who never approved of my choices as a teenager. 'Why can't you look more like Jean Watson?' (in stout brown lace-up shoes), as I sat in church, sporting the first pair of shoes I ever bought for myself, swinging them back and forth on my elegant, tiny feet, slim legs and ankles. Those white stiletto slingbacks with exquisite pointy toes marked my transition into grown-up-ness!

So, the essence of who we are; our own spirituality? How do we express that in our clothing? In his fascinating, if rather outdated and politically incorrect (1930s) The Psychology of Clothing, Flugel cites various categories of how we choose our clothes, for example; Rebellious; I refuse to reflect who I am in my clothing. Resigned; can't be bothered. Unemotional; not engaging emotions, in choice. Prudish; protective, as a monk's habit protects his virtue. Sublimated; where elements in body and clothing fuse into harmonious unity, unlike other types where there is usually unresolved internal conflict. Interestingly, he believes that women who adorn their body consciously are usually more wholly integrated! His preface also raises the correlation between psychology and spirituality - the consciousness of being perfectly well dressed may bestow a peace 'such as religion cannot give'. And he likens it to 'another Trinity' - Decoration, Modesty and Protection.

To take this a step further, paradoxically not only does the clothing we wear express the individuality of who we are but also garments themselves can influence how our limbs and other parts of our body move; of how we are able to function. High heeled shoes affect our body posture and the way we walk (I have heard this described as 'pert'); a straight tight skirt certainly restricts any movement of a vigorous nature! Uniform can help us display the behaviour of the profession it represents, e.g. a police officer or a nurse. Clergy move in long garments, demonstrating a power and grace which could not be achieved by the naked body. A solemn, measured gait expressing dignity, no need to hurry, the mind on higher things than rushing around!

Mother Teresa said she could exist with only a bucket and two saris, but she certainly could not have managed without the saris! Some of my clothes I remember as good friends to me. Linda Grant in The Thoughtful Dresser wrote that indeed some of hers have been better friends to her than some of the people she has known. She also regrets the sad invisibility of women in public generally after their fifties, whilst affirming 'raddled old ladies wearing lipstick which bleeds into the cracks, who can at least be seen. In a recession we cannot allow life to become beige!' A love of clothes and appearance can be critically judged by some as indicating a superficial character, so it is good to remember that you cannot have surfaces without depths! Theologian Angela Tilby adds that our outer and inner selves can nourish each other if we are aware of how we are perceived by others and give them the 'clues' accordingly. We may feel that it is only the knowledge of our inner core which is important, to ourselves and others, but adds that if the other cannot perceive the 'inner us', then they have no access to who we really are.

So serious stuff, amidst all the rejoicing and celebrating around our faithful garments. But here is a fitting P.G. Wodehouse chuckle, supplied by Emma:

Bertie: I say, Jeeves, as a matter of interest, what are you doing?
Jeeves: I'm sorting through these clothes, Sir. These (indicating one pile of clothes} are for repair, and these (indicating the other pile) for discarding.
Bertie: Oh, wait a second! This white mess jacket is brand new!
Jeeves: I assumed it had got into your wardrobe by mistake, Sir. Or else that it had been placed there by your enemies.
Bertie: I will have you know, Jeeves, that I bought this in Cannes.
Jeeves: (disbelieving) And **wore** it, Sir?
Sadly, we don't all have such an enigmatic sartorial adviser.

What would life be if we did not have the courage to try? Vincent van Gogh

******

Chapter 5

And then, to sing the new song of wisdom and ancient instances, and so she plays her costumed part.

Plackets and Glimpsing Through

1996 – 2003

In which I ran a retreat centre from our home called Wellsprings...completed an MA in Contextual Theology...officiated at many funerals...and LOST all my best summer clothes forever in the move to Yorkshire!...

The Fifth Age

Naked and you clothed me
i)   Glimpses
ii)   Robes
iii)   Harassing the High Hats
iv)   Wellsprings
v)   Listening to Hunger
vi)   Burial clothing
vii)   Meeting People where they are
viii)   The Red Shoes in the Churchyard
ix)   The Wet Suit
x)   Loss

Naked and you called me
xi)   Cloaks. Concealing, Protecting, Warming
xii)   Lostness and Foundness. Transcending the Boundary of Loss
xiii)   Entering the mystery. The Tallith, Jewish Prayer Shawl

Naked and you clothed me

Glimpses
Written in 2016

      Plackets are a sort of pleat in the fabric of a garment. Practically they allow a little room for expansion or manoeuvre without straining the garment, e.g. in a side seam or the centre back seam of a jacket. But they also allow a little peeping through to a layer of fabric beneath, maybe even a different colour or design when at their most subtly crafted.

      This is the period in my life when I was beginning to discern such mystery and awesome enrichment of a spiritual nature, beyond what was immediately presented, tantalizingly just beyond my reach. This was to develop later in my time in York at the Bar Convent on a course I undertook called Psychological and Spiritual Development. But it began before then, back in Bedfordshire as the children were growing and developing themselves, by my attending retreat weekends and learning to listen to God in prayer as opposed to just only wanting to tell Him and ask Him things. At that time began the discovery of finding Him/Her in the stillness; experiencing a fleeting discernment, such as I glimpsed in the flash of a kingfisher whilst with my father on the bridge over the beck behind our home recently.

Disclosure

Prayer is like watching for the Kingfisher. All you can do is
Be where he is likely to appear, and wait.
Often, nothing much happens;
There is space, silence and expectancy.
No visible sign, only the knowledge that he has been there,
And may come again.
Seeing or not seeing cease to matter, you have been prepared,
But sometimes, when you've almost stopped expecting it,
A flash of brightness gives encouragement.

Candles and Kingfishers. © Ann Lewin

.   Moments of insight came, like the kingfisher, unsought and unexpected, but as a sacred resource on which to draw beyond the moment. These glimpses began scarily to shake the journey of my life, leading me into unexpected pathways and landscapes, hitherto undreamed of and astonishing. You will be able to join me on two of these pathways. Indeed, some of you who will be reading this will have been fellow pilgrims on the way. Come along with us - taste and see.

**

So, what are some of these flashes, insights and glimpses?...

******

Robes

The two prime energies of this decade for me were Wellsprings (my retreat centre for those of any faith or none) and an Oxford Brookes MA in Practical and Contextual Theology. To be honest they were 'energies' which impacted hugely in a variety of ways on my dear longsuffering family too. It was the moment when I discovered that my ministry was no longer to be practised exclusively whilst clothed in ancient Roman style garments, stood at a lectern or in a pulpit from a lofty height. These garments do give one an air of authority and maybe do evidence having been educated for the job. Those issues are important, I do acknowledge. The other bonus to them is that it does not matter what you wear underneath. This has become a clothing issue for me now that I mainly conduct worship in a nonconformist church and sometimes even at funeral services for those bereaved relatives who do not want me to look like 'formal religion'. There is a debate within myself on all these occasions as rummaging through my wardrobe I seek to be appropriate in my clothing. I need to be respectful, discreet, not flamboyant or distracting in any way from the matter in hand. Many women officiant minsters get round this by wearing grey trouser suits or black academic gowns: I do not go down that route.

There is another theory to which I do not subscribe and that is that robes make all minsters look the same, i.e. that they do not allow the personality and individualism to shine through. That is unrealistic in my humble Reader opinion. It does not allow for the various academic hoods, scarves, drapes, embroidery, sashes, ecclesiastical badges of office, dog-collars, swinging crosses, badges of cathedral office, copes, capes, high hats and general adorning bric-a-brac. The Reader robes, whilst denoting that one is the lowliest and least of all the Anglican ministers, nevertheless ensure that you go first in any formal church procession. This is presumably because Jesus taught us that the first shall be last and the last first in the kingdom of Heaven. The Anglican Church overtly and in all humility pays homage to that in any formal procession at the very least.

Robes do become a part of one's identity. At eighteen months one of my grandsons came into our home where my robes hung on the coat rack by the door. He pointed up to them, beamed and with joy announced, 'Grandma'.

One or two more robes stories are linked significantly. I lent my first cassock to a lady priest who did not have one and I rarely wore mine. It was never returned and anyway I usually wore a white cassock alb for funerals , but if in emergency taking an Evensong in a parish church, I would wear under my surplice and scarf a long black Laura Ashley dress. Indistinguishable. But one day I officiated at a funeral and burial in a very boggy and muddy churchyard. It was for the father of a friend of mine who is a sewing and tailoring genius. 'You are never to wear that white robe thing again for a funeral in a churchyard, Ann. It gets muddy and I am going to make you a black one.'

Oh goodness. It is magnificent. Tailored to fit down the length of my body with deep cuffs on the sleeves, and darts in the back of the waist, coming to embroidered points. Down the front is a long satin stitched black shiny ribbon with tiny silk covered buttons from neck to hem. It is beautiful and precious because crafted especially for me. I have now lent it to one of my friends who is the first Reader they have ever had at York Minster.

So, yes, in our Wellsprings ministry no one wore any of these formal garments, whatever their status - nor indeed were they missed. I did personally go though many robe incarnations over the years; choir robes, Reader robes, alb, cassock, surplice, Reader scarf, academic hoods (BA, MA) and academic gowns for ceremonies, even the mortar board for Oxford (hired, of course). But in Wellsprings informal and welcoming clothes for most occasions were the norm.

**

The institutional church, however, was bound to pose a challenge…

******

Harassing the High Hats

The human being is the only animal in creation who wears clothes; that is the sign that they are made in the image of God. Lawrence Langor.

Hence supposedly the reason those medieval bishops wore two hats, to make them even higher as the closest human beings of all to their maker!

As a lay minister pioneer in the Church of England, coming from a non-conformist background, I had to learn more than one lesson the hard way. In a powerful hierarchical institution, I had to learn that maintaining the status quo at all costs seemed to be the name of the game, despite the urge to us all to 'Think

107

out of the box', amidst continuous vague mumblings from on high about moving around the structural deckchairs on the monumental liner, whilst the Titanic was in danger of continuing to sink. From my retirement status reflecting on all this, I think I was less a thinker outside the box than the jack which jumped right out of it. But I never stopped hoping that someone would listen to my lay concerns.

I went to see the play by Dennis Potter, Son of Man, and was struck that the high hats (phylacteries) worn by the Pharisees reminded me of a bishop's headwear today, and I wrote the following poem after a healing service at one of the abbeys. Why I offer it here is that there is a movement in it and a shift towards a respect for the one who was praying with me. I have never forgotten it. But that movement could not have happened if I had not first dared to express my anger.

Without wanting to be guilty of rash generalisations, expression of anger is hard for women of my generation. As sisters of a working-class household in the Fifties, we had a father who himself had been brought up to 'keep his tongue between his teeth'. To express anger was very bad indeed, if not actually sinful! Thus, there was a great deal of 'silencing' in our family; silencing, denial and suppressed rage. We read that anger is OK if expressed appropriately, but that is very difficult when there has been no prior 'rehearsal' in a safe family arena. So, I share this in the hope that anger can be seen as a passion within, being used creatively to metaphorically move mountains!

A Celebration of Healing

Some cough in the smoke of the incense,
Many hearts lift in fragrance of love.
Eyes turn to high altar whence lean…
The High Hats…Oh Heavens above.

"Please heal me of my anger," she prayed,
As their arms gently round her they laid.
Eyes flashing in anguish she knelt there;
Her rage and fury displayed.

"Lord help us to listen to others," he prayed.
He didn't. They didn't. They still don't; she swayed.
Sanctimonious deliverance, and pompous, arrayed,
He stood there and said it!

She trembled, afraid.
"The high hats I want to knock off," she confessed;
Burning with anger, by which she's possessed.

"Let her know, Lord, it is in her anger,
That her passion for you there is found.
Transform it, release it, renew it.
Help her know, Lord, her reason is sound."

A thorn in the side of the High Hats?
The grit in the oyster, a pearl?
As sun shaft pierced the arched window,
And warmed the cold stone wall.

© Sue Howard

**

And from high hats all the way down to red shoes and one of the greatest red shoes adventures of my life; indeed a risk - my retreat centre…

******

Wellsprings
Written in 2003

'...open your eyes and look at the fields; they are ripe for harvest'
John 4:35

Wellsprings began with no official imprimatur. Some of the 'kind' amongst the Anglican 'powers that be' referred to it as 'rather a maverick enterprise', certainly 'on the edge', whilst the less than kind sent letters which I could possibly sell to the News of the World one day and retire! After having a double-paged centre spread in the Diocesan magazine, See Round, one subsequent December though, it could be seen that it had matured into respectability. (Indeed currently it probably would now be vigorously celebrated as a 'creative fresh expression of being church'.) 'Maverick' was the term which initially saddened me the most, so I looked it up in the dictionary. It means 'someone who doesn't brand his sheep', so maybe that was not so far from the truth, with Wellsprings being truly and wholly ecumenical in every sense!

A figure in a parish magazine cartoon was depicted sitting in the middle of the road. The caption ran... 'You might be on the right track but you will get run over if you just stay sitting there'. I had sat for years through numerous PCC meetings going over and over a document known as the Covenant for Growth and I just knew that my model of mission was completely upside down by comparison. Suddenly I knew that for me the message was that 'Jesus went out from the temple, into the homes, lanes, the boat, by the well, on the beach etc. etc. and I have to go out too'.

So I walked away from my salary as hospital lay chaplain and we opened our home in Hockliffe as a place of hospitality and spirituality, as a Christian place to welcome those of any faith or none, and called it Wellsprings. Paul and I believed this to be very much in the tradition of the provenance of the house as a Hospital of St John the Baptist in Medieval times. Also in terms of hospitality and refreshment, it is appropriate to remember its eighteenth-century life as a roadside inn!

There were no business plans, proposals, strategies, meetings, we just did it. Six years later we had more work than we could handle. We had been much freer than a big institution to respond swiftly to need. It was allowed to evolve freely, overseen by a management committee chaired by a fellow Diocesan Reader and assisted by numerous faithful, enthusiastic volunteers, and eventually embraced by the local archdeacon.

Mailing literature only reflected the tip of the iceberg. A newsletter was published twice a year and distributed locally and more widely. Each time it would describe regular events such as Yoga, Cross Stitch, Relaxation Class, Meditation, Library Lunch, Meet and Eat suppers for the bereaved, along with Quiet days, professionals' Away Days and individual retreats. Similarly, an inviting and varied range was offered of special day workshops and courses, all led by professional and experienced facilitators – as in the following sample programme of actual weekend events. And the seasonal needs of Christmas – with feasting, music and food for body and soul – were certainly not overlooked!

The outdoor possibilities were not neglected either – taking advantage of the original 'rooms' of the layout of the Georgian acre and a half of land. This comprised a vine house, a wooded area, pond, herb garden, orchard and lawns.

WELLSPRINGS
Sample Programme of Special Events

Month One
Week One *De–Stress your life with Yoga* Jean R.
Spend a day exploring techniques to help alleviate stress in your life. Learn about the causes of stress and how to recognise symptoms. Control stress with gentle physical movements which will release tension in the body. Explore breathing, meditation and relaxation.
Week Two *Growing Old Outrageously* Janet R.
This workshop offers a fun-filled look at the lighter side of becoming 'a certain age'. Can the second half of life be better than the first? Come seeking wisdom and joy, wearing your sense of humour and comfortable clothes!
Week Three *The Quiet Painter* Revd Bruce D.
A quiet day of prayerful reflection and creative expression, using the house and gardens at Wellsprings as your inspiration. Suitable for all levels of ability including beginners.
Week Four *Schoolgirl Stories* Janet S.
A light-hearted look at old–fashioned schoolgirl stories – with some ideas to get you thinking!

Month Two
Week One *Fasting and Feasting* Jean H.
Rituals of Fasting and Feasting play an important part in the living faiths of the world. A day to look at central beliefs and the place of ritual food in the Hindu, Islamic and Judeo/Christian traditions. There will be a chance to sample Indian delicacies of Diwali and an Islamic lunch for Eid el Fitr. We will conclude by sharing a Christian feast of life and renewal.

Served in a Kaftan...

Week Two *Lanterns and Coffins* Paul N.
Discover alternative approaches to arranging a more personal funeral. This workshop day will explore woodland burial, cardboard coffins, funeral decorations such as lanterns and the releasing of balloons. We will also put together a memory box.
Week Three *An Introduction to Complementary Medicine and Stress Management* Hilary C.
What is complementary medicine and how does it work? How could it help you? How do you choose between the different therapies available. A structured day of talks and demonstrations by qualified therapists with plenty of time for questions, discussion and a chance to experience a 'taste' of a variety of therapies.
Week Four *Midsummer Soirée* Lawrence N. Master of Music, Dunstable Priory.
Come and experience the enchantment of a Midsummer evening at Wellsprings. Chamber music in the drawing room; supper in the hall; and the party in the rest of the historic house and gardens. Not to be missed!

112

Month Three
Week One *Chakras, their role in Healing and Relaxation* Gill M.
Through imagination, meditation, movement and breathing, we can become aware of these important energy centres and begin to work with them in our own healing and in sharing with others. Time for energy balancing work, strolling, reading, dozing or painting on glass!
Week Two *Discovering Celtic Spirituality through a day with St Cuthbert* Daphne C.
An opportunity to explore some aspects of Celtic Spirituality by looking at one of the most famous Celtic saints. Finding help along our own spiritual journey from the lifestyle, prayer and attitudes to the natural world of St Cuthbert.
Week Three *Story Action Workshop* Caroline P. and Grace J.
Discover a new way of thinking about ourselves and the way we adapt to situations by using fairy tales, myths and stories. Follow the twists in plot and engage with the characters for a fascinating insight into our own attitudes and relationships. Learn how to handle the dramas and frustrations of our own lives! This workshop can be tailored to meet individual needs using different stories to address themes like anger, depression, family dynamics, loneliness and abandonment.
Week Four *An Introduction to Antiques relating to the history of Hockliffe House* Ann H.
Use your powers of observation and deduction as you learn more about the fascinating history of the home of Wellsprings through antiques and bygones. Beginning with the twelfth century arch over the kitchen door. You will be led through the different periods of the house, with its spirit of healing and hospitality. Relate objects to their historical and social context and experience the ritual of Georgian tea–drinking!

Month Four
Week One *I have a Dream* Revd Roger J.
By popular demand another chance to explore how we can learn from Jung and use the experience of the dream we have. You will be encouraged to work on your own material during the day.
Week Two *Women Who Slay and Sing* Revd Judy H.
Down the ages the church has stressed the qualities of gentlemen, with submission being the crown of womanhood. The point is illustrated with stories of women such as Hannah and Mary, but there are also many Biblical women who did not fit this submissive mould. Saviours of their nation who rejoiced in violence and bloodshed and celebrated it in song and dance. Come along and hear about some of them. Light refreshments for those with stronger stomachs!
Week Three *Listen My Child* Revd Richard W.
A quiet day with the opportunity to look a little closer at the book of Proverbs, part of the Old Testament's wisdom literature, which offers reflections on the ordinary and extraordinary experiences of life.

Week Four *Traidcraft* Caroline V.
Come and admire the craftsmanship of people from all over the world. Textiles, clothing, jewellery, pottery, stationery and crafts – fairly traded and environmentally friendly and available to browse or to buy at Wellsprings. Looking for a gift for a friend or a treat for yourself, pop in for ten minutes or stay for the fashion show and refreshments and make an evening of it.

Month Five

Week One *Photography* Eileen B.
Use the lens of your camera to discover something new about God's wonderful world. Spend the morning exploring at Wellsprings, taking photographs in the house and garden. Your films will be developed while you are having lunch. The afternoon workshop will give you a chance to discuss your work and learn how to improve on your technique.
Week Two *A Day with Hildegard of Bingen* Revd Elaine C.
Discover an amazing woman! Hildegard of Bingen was born into a noble German family in 1098. She experienced God in her life from an early age and became a woman of deep prayer. A wonderfully gifted person – skilled in medicine, philosophy and music, who had haunting and disturbing visions from God. What does she have for us – nine hundred years after her birth?
Week Three *Stones.* Brenda M.
A quiet day of meditation, with silence, poetry and music, looking at stones in Scripture, from the tablets of the Ten Commandments to the stone rolled away from the tomb.
Week Four *Murder Mystery* Nemesis Community Theatre Group.
The usual peace and tranquillity of Wellsprings is disrupted by the shocking discovery of a body in the library. Time to exercise those 'little grey cells'. Come along to join the investigation and discover 'whodunit' and why.
    And many, many more.

    Food, home-cooked and served around the table, became legendary in the lifetime of this centre, recalling many stories around the life and teaching of Jesus Christ which were set in such a context. Having revisited old programmes for the purpose of this book, I am moved and even more aware of how Wellsprings gave all these facilitators an opportunity to share their expertise, creativity, passion and gift for the enrichment of the spiritual lives of so many during those years!

    A regular attender commented, 'I can only think of Wellsprings now like the pre-Raphaelite painting, *The Light of the World*, the picture in Keble College, Oxford. Every time someone rings the bell, you open the door to Jesus.' I came to recognize that He knocks in a variety of disguises!

    I reflect now that I had to draw a little apart from the riches of the church in order to rediscover them. Whilst continuing to work throughout the deanery and beyond as a Reader and ecumenically in various churches, I was discovering in humility where God is already at work in people outside the church building as well as in. Meeting people where they are, not where we think they ought to be, beginning in relationship and valuing the exchange of what we have to offer one another. This change reflects the organic nature of Wellsprings, the opportunity to be able to loosely hold that dynamic of continuity and change and the insight and understanding that the key rests with people not doctrine, in those in the church and those outside with whom God is also in relationship.

One of my secular therapists remarked that there were several 'Holistic' centres which had opened in the area around that time and had subsequently closed. She said that she had astonished herself by wondering if Wellsprings' success was due to the firm theological foundation which underpinned it, whilst not defining the way its life evolved!

In preparing this for writing, I am moved anew at how many men and women gave their time and expertise in this creative adventure. Others supported in gift, help, care and prayer. I note how many of these programme invitations begin 'discover' or an 'opportunity to explore', and we did! Thank you to all who offered so much to so many, enabling an exploration of spirituality in its wider sense, in education, experience, friendship, stillness, prayer and fun!

N.B. This is a revised and retrospective version of a presentation to Dunstable Deanery Synod on 3.3.03. (A somewhat Trinitarian code for the discerning!)

**

But, while many appreciated good food, another group of pilgrims who began to make their way to Wellsprings were mothers of young women suffering from eating disorders. These mothers came speaking of being 'at their wits' end'...

******

Listening to Hunger

From the start Wellsprings' hospitality was built on welcome and the sharing of food home-cooked on an Aga and eaten around the table. The name Wellsprings conjured up an image which most could relate to as refreshing and life giving. To Christians it is a reminder of the account of Jesus meeting the woman of Samaria at the well, as recorded in John 4, where a conversation between strangers took place and the woman was transformed. Paradoxically, however, specific research emerged contextually from the Wellsprings work with women who were presenting not with positive but with negative issues around food. The centre became a doorway through which especially the mothers entered, and a crucial debate over the complexities of body image and self-worth became possible. Mothers, who had nowhere to go other than their daughters' clinicians who were frequently judgmental of them, spoke of being 'at their wits' end'. They presented nearly as often as the other most frequent group, the be-

115

reaved. Was this evidencing a spiritual need, either consciously or unconsciously, which had drawn them trustingly to seek support from such a 'faith' centre?

Such kindly and professional help continued throughout, whenever the call arose, but a national Eating Disorder association also ran four separate day courses for parents of children or young adults with an eating disorder. Questions were answered about why, what and how; resources were suggested and offered by two experienced specialist professionals. It wasn't about clothes, but it was about that related topic, body image.

N.B. The whole study and its findings were published as my MA by Oxford Brookes University in 2003.

**

And now an oblique look at the other major area of this centre's support, bereavement…

******

Burial Clothing
Written in 2000

'Why are things never normal in this house?' asked my bemused son, on arriving home from university recently. Three cardboard coffins greeted him in the hall as he came in - a beautiful gold-painted one decorated with huge glazed autumnal leaves; a zebra; and a bookcase entwined with roses. Shortly after he arrived, we had a telephone call to announce that there were some Bed and Breakfast guests en-route. Thus, a quick panic facilitated said coffins hastily carried up the main stairs, through the bathroom, across the landing and secreted in the laundry room!

The following day, Wellsprings went to the nearby Hospice for a two day 'drop in' for staff, volunteers and Hospice at Home workers, to raise awareness of what is available in terms of alternative ways of celebrating life during a funeral or burial service. We focused particularly on the possibilities surrounding woodland burial, 'Green' funerals, and burial in cardboard coffins or shrouds.

The local bishop had recently raised the issue and the Diocese was even exploring the possibility of a consecrated woodland burial site. As a Reader, I conduct many funeral services in a year and mostly for those families on the outside or edge of the church who need especial help to discover Christian hope at this time without the burden of language and concepts which are now alien to many.

The wonder of this was vividly portrayed at the end of the day, when yes, there was a challenge. A little family came in with their small son who had not much longer to live. I sat on the floor with his mother and we talked haltingly and quietly whilst a local funeral director spoke with the father. This was for real, and eventually we felt that we had helped that young family move a little way to

116

being heard in their needs for that imminent occasion, spiritually and practically. We were together able to offer reassurance of continued care and support for that time of grief, thanksgiving and a tentative and fragile hope, whilst being conscious of their gift to us of trust at this tender moment in their lives.

N.B. Abridged from an article published in the St. Albans' Diocesan magazine, See Round.

Note: A coffin in traditional Yorkshire is known as 'the wooden overcoat'.

**

I have hopefully built up a partial picture for you of the work and nature of Well-springs and to conclude, here is an independent review when ultimately as a family we left Hockliffe House, and Wellsprings had to close...

******

Meeting People where they are
Written by Sue Howard 2004

For seven years Wellsprings has embodied a commitment to both the institutional and the 'fresh' models of church. There has always been a 'both/and' philosophy at its heart.

Those who gathered recently to celebrate seven years of Wellsprings were a living testimony to what had been written in the early days: '... the example of Jesus Christ whose ministry was spent preaching, teaching and healing outside the temple – along the road, beside the lake, in people's homes, at the

117

well... So Wellsprings offers hospitality to those of any faith or none at all'. Voice after voice echoed this experience of welcome, unconditional acceptance, renewed confidence and growth in faith/spirituality and thanks for the wonderful meringues! Is this not Eucharist?

The 'both/and' ethos was amply demonstrated as clergy, laity and those outside formal church structures gave thanks. Individuals, community teams, pastoral teams had found a creative space at Hockliffe House and re-connected with their humanity. Is this not Kingdom business?

It was recognised that, while Wellsprings' specialness reflected Ann's particular personality, experience and skills, this had not discouraged other initi-atives. People commented on the need to live out of our own particular gift-ings/humanity. Some are indeed continuing things begun by Ann, such as the Meet and Eat suppers for the recently bereaved.

So, a few key questions arise:

i)   What are the current factors that make it difficult to hear, evaluate and incorporate the lessons being learnt from those involved in fresh ways of being church?

ii)   How can the Institutional Church replicate this 'both/and' model? Note the comment from the Group recently reviewing the 1983 Pastoral Measure, "We believe new provision is needed for use on a permissive basis to allow recognition and encouragement to be given to non-parochial church and mission models."

iii)   What do we identify as 'the hoops' of the Institutional Church that some feel have to be jumped through in order to be acceptable and thus opt out of Church as a place for exploring their life journey?

**

All serious stuff, but even in extremis there could be a lighter side...

******

The Red Shoes in the Churchyard
Written in 2012

One day I found myself having to go into the office of the Cemetery Chapel in Dunstable for some query or another. This was like an inner sanctum, where the men changed clothes chameleon-wise, several times a day, from being grave diggers to cemetery chapel attendants, to gardeners or into which-ever disguise was required. Mugs were very stained, so one usually resisted the invitation of a cuppa or stoically endured on the odd occasion, because these men were your friends and made life very much easier for you.

On the occasion in question, however, I sensed a slight unease as I walked in, and glancing up above the desk where languished the saucy calen-dars and the like on the notice board, nestling in among Beds. County Council notices, rules, timetables, cartoons, pin-ups...

118

Oh no! There I am in a half page full-colour newspaper photograph. I was solemnly walking down the church path in Eaton Bray, leading the coffin procession of a legendary Luton Town footballer (personal request by the widow for me to officiate). I am of course in my Reader robes and …the red shoes. Oh dear, Disaster! A public manifestation of my bending rules on several counts. Be sure your sins will find you out. It wasn't the Red Shoes Pope in those days, or else I could also even have been considered to have ideas above my station. Perish the thought! And never let it be said! Was this a prophetic moment? We shall see. Time will tell.

This article first appeared in 'Plus', a quarterly publication by Christians on Aging.

**

And an off-duty activity with my family also entailed an unintended funny side, as you will see when you read about courage, risk and danger on the high seas in a wet suit!...

******

119

The Wet Suit
Written in 2012

Family life in all its fullness continued alongside and around The Book Castle and Wellsprings. One occasion, now remembered by those of us who were there, as one of 'courage, risk and danger on the high seas', I share now, as one of the daunting challenges of my life.

On annual family holidays for years, I had walked or perched on the cliff top at Sharpitor, gazing longingly into the Salcombe Estuary. I so wanted to be in it or on it, and not just gazing over and across and down into it. On the sparkly green/blue water would be little sailing boats tacking back and forth; cruisers and tripper boats, languorously enjoying the calm and stunning coastal views; in the stillness of the early evening, moored, softly lit craft, with the sound of conversation, laughter, chink of glass on glass, sometimes music, drifting gently up and around the cove into the gathering dusk. Here were the speed boats with semi-naked, vigorous young men crossing and criss-crossing the spume wake, their craft almost lifting and bouncing out of the water in the deep, deep cove. Even more intrepid were their water skier counterparts, also lifting and bouncing out of, and sometimes into that same deep place; bump, bump, bump, resounding around the arc of the cliffs.

But all these exploits I knew were beyond me, age-wise, fitness-wise, expertise and finance-wise. There was always, however, the Banana Boat to which I secretly and tentatively aspired, maybe one day on which to venture into that mysterious water, into that magical cove. I would be safely seated on the banana, albeit at speed, holding on to the safety handles and with someone else behind and before me. There would be a user friendly young man to tow and steer the banana.

The challenge was accepted one fateful day, with all the family slightly anxious. Paul went to the top of the cliff to watch safely over me and be reassured (he can't swim). Mark (future son-in-law) thought that he and Hannah should come with me on the banana with ditto motives. We three sauntered into the holy of holies, i.e. the back room of the water sports centre, with an air of expectancy, and there observed the rows of jaunty wet suits displayed invitingly on rails. A young man found me the largest size and left me in a curtained off area to slip into it. Well, I didn't slip into it, at all. After much very difficult, rubbery and sticky tugging and pulling onto my middle-aged body shape, I eventually emerged to a horrified Hannah and Mark. 'Mum, you've got it on back to front!' Well, how could I have known that the zip did not belong at the front? So back I went to go through it all again. Next the life jacket and floats. H'm! Somewhat unexpected. Finally, we emerged and plodded to the beach where I was asked by the young man, 'Do you mind getting wet?' What a strange question, I thought. Of course, I did not. How could I have considered going on a banana boat, around the bay and across the bar into the Atlantic in order to reach the deep, deep cove without getting wet?

120

First then, a little boat, requiring a hazardous transfer in the water onto the banana. Not a breeze for me, I can tell you. But then...oh bliss, oh joy, I am astride the bright yellow banana, holding on to my handle. The sun is blazing, the sea is sparkling, the banana is speeding at a zip-along speed, faster and faster - oh my goodness! Then the towing speed boat began its severe brake and turn, brake and turn over and over again as I clung on desperately. Which is, of course exactly what I should not have done, because my arms felt as if they were being hauled out of their sockets.

That was what they had meant by 'getting wet'. They had actually been asking me if I minded being flung off into the deep, deep cove. Nearly unconscious with fear by this time, I somehow subconsciously became aware that I had not to hold on but to let go. Over the banana I went, with watching Paul nearly sick on the cliff top, powerless to help or respond to the screaming. I tried to swim, not knowing that as I was wearing life floats I was not able to swim. I did not know that one just had to let go again, trust and float until rescued.

Our banana boat had drifted away. 'OK this is it, I am going to drown,' and then I saw Mark coming to rescue me. I do not remember what happened next but Mark tells me that he dragged me to the banana and strugglingly lifted my legs over, and all the time I was saying, 'Leave me to drown - just save yourselves.' He still married my daughter!

Paul made his way on wobbly legs down the path to the pub where he downed the stiffest drink of his life!

**

A loss of face certainly in this story leads to another story of loss. The loss of some of my very favourite clothes...

******

Loss
Written in 2015

Clothes wear out – usually the ones which have been most loved, and it is indeed sad to say 'goodbye' to them. My favourite garment of all time was 'kind to me'. It was an ankle length waistcoat, pink and grey with plackets, pockets, striking diamond design, a Fairtrade garment which eventually just frayed to bits. It could be worn over almost any outfit to its advantage; and slimming and skimming my middle-aged self also to advantage! Various garments I have had photographed in order to remember them, before I had to say a gracious celebratory 'goodbye', as I just did not have room to keep them any longer, and in the rise of the vintage clothes market in York some were welcomed to new racks, and hopefully now enjoy fresh creative lives and relationships where they continue to be celebrated.

121

But, oh dear! The trauma of the ones I actually lost. Linda Grant says some clothes mysteriously just disappear in the night, never to be seen again, but what I am to tell you now will make even strong women tremble!

I was moving North, a big intrepid adventure in my late fifties. We had always known that the several decades we spent at Hockliffe House were as mere caretakers in a long line from medieval times to today. It was winter when I moved, so my winter clothes were being packed safely in my suitcase, but my precious summer ones, collected over decades, which still fitted me, were going with the removers in a black plastic sack. You have guessed it!

There were in that sack amazing, unique garments – designer; linen; silk; Indian; calico; a maxi cheesecloth dress of the 60s; fringed, silk handmade-by-my-Mum harem trousers; a navy fisherman's smock from Salcombe in colours around collar, patch pockets and lining of emerald green, bright yellow, sky blue and red. Whenever I wore any of these with their feel, their sound, their association with exotic cultures beyond my experience, I became transported. These clothes for better or worse did shape me, I know.

Yes, they went into the landfill, accidentally put out for the bin men. By whom? I will say no more. Could I ever forgive this? I felt not. But do you know, as I write this, the loss I mourned the greatest and still do are the Andy Pandy blue and white striped dungarees. Needless to say that I will NEVER pack anything in black plastic sacks EVER EVER again.

There is a sequel to this house-moving story that I include because it is part of the whole, and some may utter darkly that it was a judgement on me that I lost my clothes! My youngest child is the most critical of his maternal upbringing. 'You were tired of being a mother by the time I was born!' It has to be said in my defence that I was a full-time mother at home for twenty years, and I am still a committed mother and grandmother all these years on.

There was a delay in Paul being able to join me full time, because Hockliffe House took longer to sell than we had envisaged. This feisty son came to me in Yorkshire for a visit. I fetched him from the station, cooked him his favourite meal, lit the fire and settled for a chat and an update on his progress - which had been spectacular and rapid in every way. He then became very serious and said he had something important to say to me. Oh dear, here it came. I recognised the signs. 'Mum, if Dad had left you behind in Bedfordshire and come up here to a new job, people would have said, "What an awful thing to do, very mean. He shouldn't have done that, how selfish!" But because it is you, a woman, people say, 'how bold, how brave, how enterprising.'

There is, however, a redemption, fellow feminists, to this sorry tale.

Several years later that son says he regrets that we do not live closer to his young, growing and evolving family.

Vindicated! Well, hopefully...

Loss in order to be found? Cloaks, coins and the healing of a prayer shawl...

******

Naked and you called me

Cloaks Concealing, Protecting, Warming

Cloaks are elegant and striking garments. I have owned several in my life, one of which graced my winter pregnancies, in those days when the glorious life burgeoning bump was considered something to disguise. There is the midnight blue velvet one with white fur collar, made originally from a remnant, worn for a marriage celebration in Whipsnade Tree Cathedral; and the full length black velvet one, lined with gold satin, worn for two of my children's Christmas weddings. Finally there is my heavy duty one (lined with red of course), needed for protection in icy blustery burial grounds. (Also occasionally, it has to be said, for icy blustery churches in rural Yorkshire, when the heating has packed up.)

There are three Bible stories featuring cloaks, which draw my interest time after time. These are Elijah in the cave, trying to hide even from God; the precious cloak of Bartimaeus; and the embracing, enfolding, womb-like cloak of the father in one of the parables Jesus told, usually known as The Prodigal Son. So cloaks in these accounts are sometimes for concealing, sometimes for protecting and sometimes for keeping warm.

Thomas Carlyle...*A man speaking of his dead wife, 'she wrapped around me like a cloak to keep the hard and cold world off me.'*

Mark 10 46-52.

Here we have an account of the healing of the blind beggar, Bartimaeus. Beggars in that particular culture were among the lowest of the low and blind beggars even lower than that. The bottom of the heap, in fact.

This passage follows the one where two of Jesus' disciples, James and John, were asking to be seated alongside him in glory, one at his right hand, the other at his left. Jesus reminds them of the calling to earn that place being not what they may have thought, and then he went on to turn the whole structure of Jewish society upside down. 'Whoever wants to be first, must first be slave of all.'

So, in that context, I invite you to look at the healing of this lowly and physically blind beggar. Immediately we see that unlike the critical, fearful Pharisees, this man did instantly recognise Jesus for who he was. His language connects directly with the unfolding of the true identity of Jesus. He shouted out, 'Jesus, Son of David, have mercy on me!' He knew who Jesus was and he knew his own need of mercy. Do we?

Many told him to be quiet. You can imagine it, can't you? We get embarrassed if someone is making a noise and carrying on, don't we? We are a society which frequently colludes in various conspiracies of silence.

But look at this lovely moment. Jesus did not rebuke him. He heard this one lowly man, even in all that crowd, and he stopped to address the crowd. 'Call him.' And look how he responds. Not ambling and shambling, shuffling and fumbling; no, 'he jumped to his feet, threw off his cloak and ran to Jesus'. I love this image of throwing off his cloak. So often I realise that we cloak ourselves, do we not, so that others cannot know us as we truly are. Do you recognise this?

Then Jesus asked him a direct question, 'What do you want me to do for you?' And he replied, 'I want to see.' 'Go,' says Jesus, 'your faith has healed you.' And then you will note that not only did he receive his physical sight. He received spiritual insight too, and 'he followed Jesus along the road'.

Here is how he did it. He recognised Jesus for who he was. He is a man who is able to watch for something he cannot see. He has sat and 'watched' in a deep and intuitive way. His hearing picks up the changing pace of what is around him, so that he can perceive instantly the identity of Jesus with a clarity the rest have not seen. As a beggar, his cloak may well have been his only material possession, but he was willing to throw it off in exchange for a relationship with Jesus. He dared to carry on speaking up even when others told him to be quiet. He responded to Jesus' call. He leapt up with energy. He threw off his cloak, that which covered him, and ran to meet the saviour of the world. The God who bends down to reach us; the God who stops for one man or woman in a crowd; for you and for me.

Do we know who Jesus is? Do we know our own need for mercy? Do we dare to name it? Can we fling off those cloaks which disguise and conceal who we really are? Dare we gaze into the loving eyes of a God who takes our face between his hands, loving and healing us into new life, new focus and new vision?

'What do you want me to do for you?'

Can we hear this invitation of Jesus for ourselves? Are we prepared to learn from the insight and response of this humble man from two centuries ago? 'Get up. He is calling you.'

**

This man laid down his cloak for Jesus. Here are stories Jesus told of being lost and found...

******

Lostness and Foundness, Transcending the Boundary of Loss...
Lost Coin from a Headdress
Luke 15: 8-10

You will have read about the trauma of a time when I lost at one fell swoop my most special clothes, never to be seen again. I invite you to share two short ac-

124

counts from the gospel of Luke, both about lostness and foundness. They both connect with clothing or adornment; the first is a story of a lost coin. It is one of three stories told by Jesus of being lost and found and thus we are told a cause for rejoicing, a party in Heaven event.

A party in Heaven?

After my retiring from the Yorkshire parishes, we initially moved house to a nearby peaceful 'idyllic' village, where it transpired eventually that rarely was anyone ever seen all day long! On our first weekend into that deserted 'silence' all my children, their spouses and our grandchildren decided to come along 'to help us move in'! In the garden there would be enormous tents, one almost bigger than the bungalow! I went to see our immediate next-door neighbours to explain that we were not going to have a rock festival or be in the habit of large, noisy, outdoor parties! Who knows what conclusions they may have drawn if I hadn't explained in advance?

It made me realise, however, that one person's party may be entirely incomprehensible to those who do not understand what is going on! And it looks as if, to the scribes, Pharisees and others, who would not listen to what Jesus told them 'was going on' in the Bible story, that Jesus was having celebration parties with all the wrong people.

So, I invite you to explore with me the story of the lost coin. Coins were worn around the head of a married woman in that culture, part of her savings or dowry, and thus to have lost it was a personal and financial disaster. Imagine the impact of such stories on those who felt not good enough for the legal Jewish experts, the righteous who did not believe they needed to change from their 'superior ways'. How would the 'lost' have heard Jesus' message of hope for themselves?

Jesus tells them, I love looking for you and I celebrate finding you! How do we hear it for ourselves today? Is there a step Jesus is calling us to take now? Is there a place where we are hiding from his forgiving, healing love? Have we by accident, carelessness, apathy, rather than by deliberate fault, rolled into a dusty corner maybe? Jesus speaks about his joy in healing those lost places, in a loving way, yes, but also in challenge.

Someone else he challenged was the woman with the long-standing blood issue. He didn't just turn and go on his way urgently to where he had been summoned, but stopped a little longer and called her out of the crowd. A beckoning, inviting Jesus, 'Come a little further with me.'

The Woman with the haemorrhage touches the Prayer shawl of Jesus.
Luke 8: 43-48

Some readers will know the significance that for the Jews of the time, this woman because of her chronic issue of blood would have been considered unclean. This woman had no status at all because of her long-standing complaint. That and death, which Jesus was also going on to 'touch' in the healing of Jairus' daughter, were just about the most contaminating and untouchable cir-

125

cumstances. And yet here was Jesus, engaging in both. This woman had carried her shame for years. When it says she will have spent all she had, it is likely that therefore all those coins of her savings and dowry had gone. This is her last chance and she dares to go for it. Here is a woman who has been made by others to feel shame. Yet here is a woman of faith. Here is a woman of courage.

This woman dared to approach and touch him. However, she does it in a crowd where she hopes no one will notice. And yet, Jesus knew. He asked, 'Who touched me?' Jesus shares his very self with her, with his own energy and power, he shows as well as tells her that she is not unclean, not shameful. He exposes the lie to which she has been exposed for so long.

We all have issues of frailty which sometimes we have carried much of our lives. Shames which we have carried inappropriately sometimes. Dumped on us by others or even scapegoated perhaps? Or things we do or say, patterns of behaviour and response from which we never seem able to get better or help ourselves. Why do we do it? What on earth am I doing here again? Maybe that is it. What on earth? Thy Kingdom come on earth as it is in heaven.

She went to Jesus. He saw into her heart as he sees into ours.

Yes, he healed her. The issue ceased. But wait! Oh help, he exposes her. Her worst fear. He stops in the crowd, turns and challenges her. He had healed her physically, but he did not stop there. He calls her on to heal her inner soul too. To make public that here is no woman of shame. When the woman saw she couldn't remain hidden, she came up trembling, and fell down in front of him. She told him in front of everyone why she had touched him, and how she had been healed instantly. 'Daughter,' said Jesus 'Your faith has saved you. Go in peace.'

Can this woman inspire us today? Can we learn from her, in that she did not lose her hope, her courage, and her faith? Now going to Jesus, what she did lose was her sense of shame. That shame which she had carried inappropriately for so long. When the lost in soul are not only found, but turn away from that which has kept them 'prisoner' from their God-given freedom, that is when there is a party in Heaven going on! The angels are joining in and we are invited to that party too! Are you going to respond to that invitation?

**

We now encounter the tallith and its inspirational significance today…

******

Entering the Mystery. The Tallith. Jewish Prayer Shawl.

From *Leaving the Bed Unmade*. Maxine Silverman, based on Numbers 15: 38
As the Sabbath begins, I put on my prayer shawl,
Not when my work is done but
'as if my work is done'.

126

Once I do that, I am aware of the presence of God.
There is that pristine privacy. I can say those words
That my heart desires and my soul requires.
The air inside that tallith changes.
First of all, it's no longer air, it's breath.
It warms with the energy of healing and the presence of the Shekinah.
Wrapped in layers of warm breath and soft grey wool
And when you emerge, who knows who you will become.
Stop.
As though your work is done.
Shabbat, shalom.

The Lord will lay bare his Holy arm in the sight of all nations.
Isaiah: 52: 10

I was once entrusted by Margaret and Alan Gilliam with a loan of some traditional Jewish clothing, to help appreciate the significance of its colour and design. I felt privileged to exhibit it as a rare, rich resource at a workshop I conducted on the Spirituality of Clothing at St. Bede's Pastoral Centre in York. Margaret writes:

'My fascination with Palestine Costume began many years ago when I helped with an exhibition which looked at the customs and costumes of Palestine in order to understand some of the things Jesus said, as recorded in the gospels. I grew to love the jackets and dresses, with their rich embroidery and deep significance. Over the years I have been given costumes from several different villages, and I use them to give talks at local church groups.

'I recently began to view this resource, however, in a new light. I went to Palestine to work with the local farmers to harvest their olive crops, and began to appreciate that the costumes I had been given help to piece together the

127

history of the villages before 1948, when the people found themselves homeless and forced to become refugees in foreign lands and other parts of their own country, cut off from their inheritance. Their significance has taken on a completely new meaning, and I treasure them, knowing that they may one day be used to help us remember a forgotten nation, living in exile'.

The photo on the previous page demonstrates the large pointy sleeves of a traditional garment, which I was delighted to discover could be rolled up above the elbow and secured so that work could be freely undertaken. My interest increased on hearing that it is a reminder that God 'rolled up his sleeve to work with us' in the Incarnation; the prophecy of the sending of his own son to be the saviour of the world. 'The Lord will lay bare his Holy arm'.

What we wear and how we wear it matters. In terms of spirituality clothing has always been an integral part of the Jewish faith and culture. It is inconceivable for anyone to turn up at the Synagogue looking a mess!

******

Chapter 6

The sixth stage shifts into yet a new melody to be composed, with the body now managing sans oestrogen, with spectacles on nose: the youthful hose now somewhat too snug a fit.

Patches, Darns and Frayed Ends

2004 - 2011

In which I moved to Yorkshire as a pioneer...experienced the richness and joy of ministry in three rural, village communities (being spoken of as the 'vicaress')...encountered unusual clothes adventures...and I am stripped.

The Sixth Age

Naked and you clothed me

Naked and you called me

Naked and you clothed me

A Confusing Pioneer
Written in 2010

*'I think at any rate,' said he, 'that it is safer to run no such risk. A very lady cu-
rate! I might perhaps essay to rule, but a curatess would be sure to get the better of me.'* Anthony Trollope. *Barchester Towers.*

After seven years of Wellsprings, with all its freedom to evolve organically, and 23 years of family life (which also evolved organically), we had to
make a fairly major change to our life-style and sell Hockliffe House, our glorious
family home and the place of hospitality for hundreds over the years we had
been there. I returned to ministry in the established Church, amazingly into an
official House for Duty post for three village churches in Yorkshire. Awaiting my
interview in a historic church in Micklegate, York, I was aware, whence I do not
know, of hearing awesomely and totally unexpectedly a voice, 'I have called you
to this place'. My interviewer looked at my Wellsprings experience and said,
'This is just what we need here.' I am not sure it was in retrospect, because the
role I was appointed to and developed eventually became too unorthodox at that
time for the Institution. 'Just go and love the people,' he said, and I did! And left
over seven years later, being told, 'You have gone native'!

This was a pioneering post to which to be appointed as a Reader, or
lay minister, it was one of the first in fact. At fifty-seven, this was an exciting
challenge to me and especially as it was 'off up north' into Yorkshire, a place to
which Paul had always felt drawn and yet we had never explored. Subsequently
he discovered that his ancestors had lived nearby for over 500 years. However I
dared do it, though, I shall never know. As a woman, lay and from the South, I
was certainly up against all the odds!

In the largest of the three villages, we were blessed in still having a
Post Office/café/village shop. I found working there in the early hours (7.00-
9.00am), cleaning and putting out fresh vegetables, bread, milk and just generally preparing a welcoming environment for the day's trade, became part of my
ministry of hospitality, but to a largely different sector of the community; fisher-
men coming for their day licences to fish in the Swale; builders working on
houses and projects coming for their breakfast; children waiting for the school
bus for their sweets. My mop and bucket became part of my stock in trade and
a source of amusement in the village. (And also at home where I had rarely ever
used one!)

In the churches we periodically held community based services. For
example, a Thanksgiving for Community Trade; 100 years celebration of the
opening of the Swing Bridge spanning the River Swale; the village/church clock
and Time, and so on. But formal worship was important to this rural community
too and eventually I re-established a choral Book of Common Prayer Evensong

which became almost our best attended service. The links with the Church of England Voluntary Aided School were key to the church's community links, with a small team from the churches visiting regularly with Godly Play and Open the Book (Bible story dramatic presentations). When I left, a nine-year-old wrote to me with, 'you made us feel part of the story'.

As a pioneering role it carried its own confusions. The people of the communities were very accepting of my slightly unusual role because, they said, 'We see 'er about.' That is what counted for them in that it showed that I cared for them, and likewise they welcomed and cared about us, a couple and family 'from the South'. But the role was a challenge, not only naturally for me but also increasingly for the hierarchy. Their message seemed, 'be imaginative and creative, but don't disturb me'. The local clergy especially, under the leadership of a conventional rural dean, were not prepared for it and, woven into the fabric of the great joy of the role for me, as the work in our three village churches grew and flourished, ran threads of pain and confusion.

**

Well, by its very nature a pioneer's pilgrimage is never straightforward, is it? You don't necessarily know where you are going, when you have arrived or indeed if you will ever be safe to return. So, look out now for patches, dams and frayed ends. Meanwhile, the meeting of the patchwork velvet coats…

******

The Patchwork Coats

The new challenge. One spring–like February day, I had beetled up the M1, M18 and A1, slowly and carefully because both my cats had eaten their way in desperation out of their cardboard cat carriers by the time I had travelled but four of a two-hundred-mile journey, into the land which signposted towns and cities which hitherto I had only ever known as the names of football teams. Chesterfield, Doncaster, Rotherham, Sheffield. The other enigmatic sign which kept manifesting was 'The North'! How mysterious was that!

Joined by Paul the next day, we were told there was to be a choral concert in the church and would we like to go? They were to perform works by Byrd and Fauré, amongst others, in that ancient and distinctive sacred building. Of course we would! How wonderful to find music and a choir of the standard of the St Paulinus singers in a small village in rural Yorkshire.

As the evening approached, a mild panic set in around us. There was a power cut; hence no organ, lighting or heating. I grew to find this sort of emergency fairly familiar but all dealt with in an impressively stoical spirit by the church hosts. Mercifully the village hall was free, so a decision was made to relocate the concert, but much consternation from the musicians about the

132

church letting them down as there were 'hopeless acoustics in the village hall', etc!

It did not disappoint, and that February evening Paul and I left the village hall hand in hand, as the snow was falling in big fat flakes. And I had met Lindsay! There we were after the concert, 'recognising' each other in our patchwork velvet coats. Thus began an exciting, creative musical relationship which brought much to the parishes in subsequent years with innovative, passionate and spine tingling music in concert and liturgy. That first night was a signpost for the way our work together would develop so unexpectedly – not so much how God was working in the church buildings, but how He/She was at work already in the community outside the restrictions of the regular church worship and liturgy? It prompted not the 'opening of the box', the established church cliché of the era, but the unlocking of the lid, the out-popping of the jack *from* the box and the exchanging osmosis passing to and fro through the ancient walls.

Through this instant recognition of each other via our outward clothing reflecting our inner spirituality, creativity and love of colour, our relationship grew to encompass the formation of a choir of local singers who did not attend regular church worship. New music was composed; new words written. Many such events included:

i)   A North Yorkshire County Council annual service with Archbishop Sentamu on the drums, to conclude my year as Chaplain to this council (he said we sang Syia Hamba like proper Ghanaians, and for the anthem we performed 'MYST', written by Lindsay and accompanied by Janet Fulton, from the Halle Orchestra, on marimba).

ii)   Musicians and singers coming in to the church and enriching the liturgy and worship, especially at Easter and Christmas.

iii)   A performance of The Crucifixion, one of the cycle of Medieval York Mystery Plays, on a cart in York combined with the village Drama group HADDS.

iv)   A marriage blessing in a wooded garden in the parish.

v)   Another completely new Mystery Play written and composed by Nick and Lindsay Ibbotson around the celebration of the Abolition of Slavery, one Good Friday. Read this report from a Diocesan publication:

'On Good Friday in 2007, St. Peter's Church, Brafferton saw a newly composed Mystery Play and musical. Lasting about an hour, the audience/congregation of a full church heard gospel songs and spirituals, very much as they would first have been sung. It was especially written and produced in celebration of the anniversary of the abolition of the slave trade, and yet also offered a powerful reflection and challenge to the Christian church today, being about human weakness, betrayal and denial. The local drama group and the village Youth Gospel choir - Scandalized - with young musicians on drums, saxophone, guitar etc. came together to offer this unique, startling and thought-provoking event'.

The drama took place in the chancel in various settings through history until modern day. In every scene a humble, silent figure, (myself) watched and waited. In one scene she was a serving wench in an inn; in another a TV cam-

era person; In another a bishop's chaplain, and finally her identity was revealed at the pearly gates! (Entertaining angels unaware?)

The preacher (me again) for the Easter Morning service was challenged by author and composer to offer a sermon in response to this unfolding drama. (No pressure then.)

People left the church on Good Friday, the majority of whom were not regular church attenders, saying. 'It made me cry.' 'It sent shivers down my spine.' 'So powerful.' 'I shall never forget the singing.'

...and all because two patchwork coats had 'recognized' each other a few years earlier.

**

And another very special coat was about to be gifted to me...

******

The Purple Velvet Coat

As narrated earlier, my swish new coat in the early 1970s was described by a friend as 'Very Ann Bowes, but I wouldn't be seen dead in it'. Then in my late fifties a local senior clergyman remarked to some of his congregation, 'Ann isn't going to be ordained. One of the reasons is that her clothes aren't suitable!' (Thomas Carlyle wrote all those years ago about women in distinctive clothing being frequently in trouble.)

So, at seventy, as I keep up the same tradition, my full length, purple velvet coat is distinctive enough to be 'willed', at their request, to a wide variety of eager strangers, ranging from a lady in a North Yorkshire rambling party, met in a tea shop on my way to see the bishop (yet again), to a fellow alto met twice a year in the deanery choir, to a shop assistant on 'cheese' in the M&S Christmas rush. Even son-in-law Lorenzo was moved to astonishment as he met me at Pisa airport in it! (Almost impressed!) I was in the farmhouse kitchen yesterday of a family of gifted artists and craftsmen and women. Their sculpture, crafted pottery, fabric and ironwork designs are stunning, unique and memorable, and even they loved the coat.

In fact, there is, of course, a story behind the provenance of this magic garment. I just throw it on over whatever else is underneath and people stop me in the street time after time to remark on it. One member of our excellent book group, intelligent, discerning and humorous (as are more than a few in the book group; this group encourages me to slip between covers I would not hitherto have dared to venture) did say that in the wearing of the magic purple coat I had encouraged people to wear their very best for everyday!
And here is its story...

One night I had gone to bed about 9.30pm and the phone rang. It was a young woman in distress from way up beyond Newcastle. She had been anx-

134

ious that her mother in my village parish hadn't been answering the phone for two days. (She did go to ground now and again, it has to be said.) She asked if I would call in tomorrow first thing. 'No,' I replied, 'I will go now.' It is true that though technically part-time in that place I was truly on call, like an old-fashioned 'vicar', 24/7 if I was not on holiday. It was an awkward situation as no one else, other than the boiler man who lived in York, had a key to Molly's house, as I was the only other person who had ever been allowed in her home at all.

The sad outcome was that Molly had indeed died, and the tragic evening unfolded. The local carpenter had come earlier to help me establish what had happened. (He then walked me home at midnight, after a strong brandy at the churchwarden's establishment!) So discreet, so just there for whatever was required always, and I still salute him for that night. I then of course had to ring the daughter.

That story of shock and sadness did not end there. Paul was away but my daughter was staying for the night at my house, with two of my grandsons asleep in the back garden in tents. None of them knew I had gone out. At about 11.30pm the undertaker hammered on my front door while I was still out. He was in his undertaker's garb, explaining discreetly to a surprised Hannah who he was, although omitting to explain the circumstances, and handed over a key to pass on to me. He then quietly left, got into his black private ambulance and drove off into the night. Oh my goodness. Not exactly a routine scenario, especially for the young campers!

Now the coat. Molly's daughter duly came with it to my house in the course of the next few days, because she had found it in her mother's wardrobe and thought I might like it. Another 'Oh my goodness' moment! What serendipity. Unbelievable. I have officiated at over 900 funerals in the course of my ministry, but never before or since been given such a magnificent gift. It is extra special because I feel I wear it for she who did not have the confidence to wear it herself. And even more special, that it is much admired...for Molly.

One day it will be bequeathed fittingly as a thank you to a particular someone for her love, kindness and inspiration in practical and spiritual matters!!

N.B. Hannah has just rung and I reminded her of that occasion. She recalled how astonished Joshua was and of how he has never ceased to be astonished about what went on in my ministry in that village! Dealing with these things didn't come in my ministry training or the contextual Theology MA; nor how to deal with a man going wild with a shotgun incidentally either! But that would be a whole new story, not told here.

**

The purple velvet coat was given me to keep. Here is a story of a garment which was 'on loan' to me; equally a gift for the moment...

******

135

The Borrowed Dress. Whoops!
Written in 2014

A long visit is planned to Emma and Lorenzo on 'the mount of olives' in Tuscany in July. I know there will be blistering heat, with severe agonies whilst being eaten alive by mozzies. Staying next door, I can't work out how to have the shutters open in the *casa,* in order to be able to let in a whisper of air whilst keeping the mozzie nets firmly shut. That I have discovered to be one of life's little mysteries kept from those who are born and raised in more moderate climes. I had my instructions from the owner of the house. 'Be careful what you use or sit on in there because there are priceless antiques in my little house. Do not use the drawing room as there is a hornets' nest in the chimney! The shutters, blinds and windows are very fragile.'

As I packed to depart I was in a mild panic for all these reasons and also because I had nothing suitable to wear for this forthcoming weather. If I could find it, though, just one item would be OK as I could wash it and dry it on the line in minutes each evening while the crickets are making their glorious racket, the lemony candles burn on the loggia, and the red wine slips relaxingly down.

ZZZZZZZZZZZZZZZZZZZZZZZZZZZZZZZZZZZZZZZZZZZZZZZZZZZZ!

Oh goodness, here come the mozzies.

And there is always a last cricket – just one left who carries on long after the others have settled down into the fragrant warm blanket of the Tuscany dark.

Anyway, back in Brafferton before I went, I am bemoaning my lack of a suitable dress with my sartorially-wise friend Chrissie, and she happened to be wearing the ideal garment. Blindingly white cotton with short sleeves, midcalf length and loose. I hesitatingly remarked, 'Your dress is just the sort of thing I have been looking for, exactly what I need, but have I been able to find anything like this? NO!'

'Well, borrow this,' she offered. 'I have had it nearly 30 years and I live in it when it's warm here.' I wasn't at all sure whether to accept, remembering 'Neither a borrower nor a lender be' and all that. And it was PLAIN as YET unmarked white, even after all those years. It is so precious to her. What if I lost my case at the airport? What if I spilled anything on it or down it?

'No, there is nothing you could possibly spill on it that does not come out. Chuck it in the machine. Never even needs ironing.'

I allowed myself to be tempted, always a mistake! O.K. here we go! Nervously and in trepidation I took it, packed it and wore it. Being very careful, hopeful and eventually too jolly complacent.

Splash went the olive oil into the balsamic vinegar dressing – a dark brown stain slowly trickling its way in a great dark brown rivulet all down the yoke and on into the skirt. Oh, grief and lamentations and complete panic. I'm on my own now on this mountain side as Emma and Lorenzo have ironically disappeared urgently to London. I tried washing – no. I tried bleaching it in the sun – no. I tried soaking overnight – no. Over and over I did it. I went down to the village shop (Alimentaire) where the previous year I had been mistakenly accused of shoplifting, to try and request a product to take out stains; bit of a language barrier. No.

However will I own up to this?

I had actually gone out to look after Emma but on her return, three days later, she took both me and the dress in hand. 'It will be OK, Mummy, we just have to soak it in bleach.' 'No. No. It might fall apart and disintegrate,' I replied in horror. 'Trust me,' she said, 'One cup full in a large sink of water. Soak for an hour, then wash.'

Hallelujah, it worked. And now I can tell all!

**

On to another village character, and her distinctive life and garb...the mole catcher...

******

The Mole-catcher, Skirts and Wellies

My first pastoral visit was to an outlying farm and I was beginning to congratulate myself on being a sort of ecclesiastical James Herriot, when the farmer came out and thrust me in front of a delivering ewe and told me that, as I was going to be the 'vicar 'ere', I had to get some decent wellies and some trousers in which I could more easily get over fences. I then watched fascinated as he was both strong and firm but also kind and encouraging to this struggling ewe. Over time, I learned that sheep cannot thrive on their own without a shepherd. They can't find all the food or water they need without occasional help and guidance. They cannot shed their fleece, which could otherwise become burdened with ticks, mites, seeds, vegetation and insects without a shepherd to shear it. Of all animals, it is the one with no natural defence against predators. It can't get up if it lies down and rolls over. If it is left there (rigwelted, the farmer tells me) without the vigilance of a shepherd, it will die. Isn't that interesting in terms of Jesus and the relational model?

Here was the modern shepherd who continued to fight a losing battle with trying to make me a more suitably clothed 'vicar' (even his beautiful daughter once presented me with a pair of old Milk Marketing Board wellies), but he and his glorious countrywoman wife I now consider to be amongst my greatest friends in this magnificent land of the shepherds.

On that first day the shepherd's wife came out to join in helping the struggling ewe, and between all three they finally produced a live and wriggly lamb, after which I was invited into their Aga-warmed farmhouse kitchen for a coffee. I had never seen anywhere like it before; lamb feeding bottles all mixed up with awaiting washing up, casseroles prepared for later, piles of farm paper-

137

work, jars of honey from the bees, a large cake ready for the WI and then in the middle of all this on the shelves on the otherwise cluttered dresser were the most beautiful Faberge style hand-painted goose eggs. 'How incongruous is that,' I thought. But no, Sally was an enigma too, which is why she endeared herself to me from the start.

Be more suitably clothed!

She is also the local mole-catcher for a wide area of our locality. As soon as those soft soil humps appeared in garden, churchyard, farm and field, she would be there, cheerful as ever with her terrifying tools of the trade. Scurry away in your underground tunnels moles, because she never fails! As she drives around she also plants bulbs, clothing the roadside verges, which grow to be a picture the following year of daffodils and snowdrops. Armed with trowel and bucket she does her rounds in her muddy boots and trousers and a very old green barbour of bulging pockets; a sight to behold. I smile wryly to think later that day she will probably be in Bradford, entranced by the ballet!

And when it was time for me to leave the parish, the following note appeared from this extraordinary lady.

Your last Sunday was wonderful, both the morning and the evening, and especially Paul's chosen words. In return I have been thinking, on my agricultural travels, of how I would liken you metaphorically – and the result was a worm! Sorry, don't squirm (I'm good at rhyming…), as nobody (I.e. the Diocesan hierarchy) likes a worm very much – but farmers simply love them. They work wonders for the soil, which in turn yields good grass, which then yields plentiful

138

milk, cheese, meat and so forth – in fact everything that the Lord said he would provide, if we look after things well. I know my garden needs a good worm or two – as do the birds.

But what does a worm live on? If ever there was a creature placed on earth for the good of all mankind, then this is it. It doesn't matter how much muck you throw at it, or give it a drought or a soaking – it will continue its work regardless. Its multiple arches/hearts must be a help. And if chopped in half, the portion with the head can even survive.

I showed her this account in case she wanted to comment. She told me her school motto, Spe Optima, or in her words, 'Just muck in and hope for the best', which was how she has lived her life. She says she is blessed with endless patience and perseverance, much needed attributes for a mole-catcher.

In these parishes I lived and breathed the land and harvest, day by day. I was throughout the year brought all the fruits of the harvest, sometimes just finding them on my doorstep, not necessarily knowing whom to thank; fish, logs, partridges, vegetables, fruit, asparagus mis-shapes, sacks of potatoes and carrots. I was explaining all this to the new vicar who had been sent to supervise me and minister as a priest to the flock! 'The people will love you and take you to their hearts,' I explained. I told him about all these gifts of abundance. There was another priest in the room at the time, and he looked quizzically at the new man. 'No,' he said. 'It isn't like that at all. I have been a priest near here for 30 years and I have never had anything.'

Bing. Bong...The front door bell rang, and in came my mole-ing friend in her mole-ing and plucking-and-drawing-game-for-The-Hall clothes, holding a large plastic box with blood dripping down the side and full of raw meaty morsels. 'Could you use up these spare partridge breasts, Ann?' I rest my case.

This poem I wrote for the village magazine in celebration of the asparagus bounty:

Ode to the Asparagus
Asparagus is *grown for us,*
Up at Pasture Lane.
The misshapes are the best for us;
The ones which missed the rain.
Quiches, soups and buttery spear,
Eat them, freeze them,
Never fear.
Worry not about the pee,
It's all part of the way you see
We know that it is Spring again,
As evidence goes down the drain.
Poking up all green and pointy,
Fat and thin and fern so dainty.
Lambs are hopping;
Asparagus cropping;

Strawberries, raspberries then are next,
Sally and Richard,
Now a rest?
Thank you.

**

But wellies were never my own footwear of first choice...

****

Spotty Dotties

I don't wear shoes or slippers indoors ever. Bare-foot just seems right and comfortable. I did read on one occasion that in some places in Eastern cultures, it is important to feel in touch directly with the ground, to such an extent they sense that to don footwear would be like walking around with blindfolds on one's feet. Yes, I can relate to that.

I am blessed with one advantage of my body shape and size, which is having small feet, Size 3. I do not consider this an advantage to do with any male fetish in such matters (e.g. foot binding in the East in former unkind days!) but simply that I get the most marvellous shoes in sales! Especially I loved a pair of red shoes in times past, just flat ballet pumps.

I must be one of the few people in our culture who does not wear trainers EVER! I am not sure why that is, but I think they are too reminiscent of football boots for me, which is probably why I shun them. I rarely wear high heels, although I do possess a pair or two for formal occasions. I have some sensible black flat comfortable Clarks shoes in which to walk to the pub with our grandchildren on dry days, boots for the wet days and wellies of course for the mud. Emma sends me lovely soft handmade leather ones from Morocco now and again, with glorious pointy toes.

I have, however, made a great discovery in my late middle age (getting towards elderly, you understand) and they are called 'Spotty Dotties'. They are flat and totally impractical and unsuitable in every way. You can't polish them because they are suede. You can't get them wet because the insides stain one's feet if you do. They wear out quite quickly and can't be repaired because no self-respecting Yorkshire cobbler will repair them. But oh my goodness, the colours! They can be teal with large purple dots (about the size of a £2.00 coin), navy with red, navy with pale blue, brown with tan, turquoise with fuchsia and any other combination you can imagine. Imported from Egypt in an altruistic move to help support local craftsmen, these come by catalogue at an exorbitant price, but in my size they are an astonishing end of season bargain every time, several pairs for the price of one! Last season I acquired two pairs of a new design, a stripey one hinting of a zebra in silver and dark grey, and one like a tiger in orange and brown.

140

They serve me well enough and I enjoy them!
Always more shoe adventures to be discovered!

Much more suitably shod!

**

But the antipathy to football doesn't extend to all the members of my family...

******

The Tribal Roar and the Scarves
Written in 2014

The first spiritual want of a barbarous man is decoration. Thomas Carlyle

On our wall a framed colour newspaper photograph depicts about eighty men crushed together - all with arms careering wildly around their heads, punching fists in the air - mouths wide open in a frozen roar of terrifying magnitude you could almost hear it still! In horror, I am told my husband and eldest son are a part of that grimacing, terrifying demonstration of ...what? Fear, anger, threat? One was put in mind of primitive peoples who make themselves look astonishingly fierce in order to daunt their enemy, with masks, paint, feathers, tusks and the like!

141

But no...hang on a minute, these men are in Birmingham, the Midlands, England, all wearing blue and white tribal garments of varying descriptions, hats, scarves, etc. And I later learn they are cheering! This is a celebration. A goal has actually been scored by their team! (Not a regular occurrence, it has to be said.) But as our eldest son explained... *Incidentally – and it may not be relevant or of note to you – it was a split second after a last-minute equalizer away at Villa in the Blues/Villa derby, the game of games, after being 2-0 down and seemingly out. That is why it was an extra special/intense moment and a particularly nice thing to capture and have? I'm sure you understand!*

I pass this souvenir photograph now and then, gracing the walls of our families' domestic dwellings, and remain in awe and wonder that triumph and aggression can look so alike!

**

And speaking of 'last minutes', I mark the closing stages of two crucial factors in my life. First a couple of tributes to my aged mother beginning with her experience of regret on my father's reaching retirement age...

******

From the Pattern Book

After my mother's death whilst my sisters and I carefully and respectfully tried to process her clothes and effects, we found the following poem in her evocative and distinctive handwriting. It was tucked into a knitting pattern book:

142

This is me at sixty-three
Endowed with boundless energy;
I want to work. I need the money;
Being retired is not all honey.
I miss the customers in the shop,
Where I worked on Saturdays, non-stop.
My husband is at home with me,
And I certainly love his company:
But I am not ready to stagnate!

We felt a little sad at this discovery because ultimately it transpired that she was to have nearly thirty years of life yet still to live, and never really came to terms with not being fully engaged in the outside arena. But she did carry on knitting socks and jumpers for Dad and indeed for all her children and grandchildren and even her great grandchildren. My father says he never wore a pair of 'bought socks' all the time he was married, about seventy years.

**

Then her cry of outrage (aged 86) at modern casual attire...

******

Bring back Busts and Waists

My mother's letter published in the Shrewsbury newspaper c.2010 (aged 86)
Recently, I spent three quarters of an hour waiting in the foyer of a busy supermarket and what a revelation that was.

It was a damp, dull, cold day and the trail of customers reflected that, and there were dozens. What a mess we have become in appearance. The ladies mostly were in the rig of the day, black polyester trousers, shapeless, faded jeans topped mainly with a short top, generally padded like part of a duvet instead of a nice long warm coat.

Hair either short back and sides or straight, tatty and lank. None of your thick stylish styles, shiny and so becoming of past years, no lipstick or make up at all to add to the appearance.

Then the men, what a shower they were. Half didn't look too fresh, no nice crisp shirt and tie and sports jacket, creases in the trousers or polished leather shoes, but stupid base-ball caps worn by old men who should know better.

Why has our dress sense gone out of fashion? Most women should never wear trousers anyway, they do not have the figures and the trousers do not fit correctly, never tailored, well rarely.

143

We need a real shake-up in our style of dress, and colour – it was all too drab. Even people's expressions were miserable, reflecting how they must be feeling, and little wonder.

What about the way little girls are dressed these days? There they were with skirts half way down their little calves, and short jackets instead of long warm coats, looking like little waifs. Granted most had warm tights but that is not enough in the winter and yes, the argument would be 'well, they arrive in cars'. Where are their hats, gloves and scarves for the times when they are exposed to the elements, which would be good for them anyway?

Everyone is so busy. Oh come on, that is nothing new, we have ladies in our village who have reared more than a dozen children, each without modern equipment, which is a must these days, and had to make do and mend, cook and bake and sew and knit when the children were in bed at night, no television viewing for them.

Life is what you make it generally, so let us have a re-think and be eternally grateful for what we have. Bring back busts, waists and svelte figures in ladies' dresses, instead of men's gear so prevalent these days; the most attractive lady who came through those doors was wearing a nice skirt and boldly patterned tights, super!

**

And this section terminates with the end of my formal ministry. I mark it here by a nostalgic homage to my favourite clothing friend in that work…

******

The Wearing and Stripping of Alb

When you read my grave clothes chapter, you will see that I intend my now redundant alb to continue to accompany me on my journey to the celestial realms! Will that be my final subversive act? Only time will tell.

Virginia Wolfe suggests that there is, *'much to support the view that it is clothes which wear us and not we them.'*

That is certainly true of my alb, which housed me, as another skin, in my formal former Reader ministry of thirty years.

Ironically, the psychologist Flugel likens the way we dress to 'another Trinity', decoration, modesty and protection; and yes, my alb is the garment which was one of my trusty clothing friends, accompanying me in roles which I still find hard to believe I was credible in; yet at the same time, protecting me with the authority of the institution; in theory at least evidencing modesty in that it removed outwardly any individuality of expression in personal clothing and was the backdrop for decoration with stole or scarf. In appearance it can best be described as a long white nightie, with full-length, loose-fitting sleeves. It is worn over one's normal clothing. It doesn't matter what you wear underneath, or how

144

fat or thin you are, as it is voluminous, so you can just slip it on over whatever, and immediately you are respectable! My alb wasn't mine to begin with; it was left to me by a departing woman priest colleague, as she returned through the sky to her homeland.

Alb goes to funerals

Because of confidentiality issues, I can share little here of the rich and privileged funeral ministry I have been entrusted with by families who require, for their loved ones, 'Something not too religious, but not Humanist'. To serve in this way has been my passion in ministry. I hope, but will never know, that my work with these families has been reflected by one man's words when he came to see me the following day. 'You did my Mum's funeral yesterday to a crematorium full of unbelievers, but we all came out with some hope.'

However, one late afternoon after such a service, at the end of the Day Before, rather than the Night Before Christmas, I was exhausted, with family commitments, work responsibilities, and worship leading yet to come. I was having a quiet moment, still in my alb, walking in the garden of the Crematorium after a particularly challenging funeral. How could it not be challenging on that day of all days? Suddenly there was a gasp as a couple came round the corner of the wall and saw me. One of them said, 'Oh God, I thought you were an angel!' Then, why oh why did I say these words? So unprofessional! I must just have been tired and in 'another place in my head'. I replied (the hurt of decades obviously), ' No. I never was chosen at school to be an angel. I never had any aspirations to be Mary in nativities, but I longed to be an angel in a glorious sparkly dress with wings and a halo. But I was only ever a shepherd with a tea-towel round my head!' Horrified, I looked at them...but the man, bless him, laughed and said, 'Well you've grown up and out-aced them all, haven't you?' One of my greatest Christmas gifts ever!

Another moment of grace from the bereaved was following a funeral at which I officiated in York for one of my retail tradesmen. The Crematorium was fuller than I had ever seen. Mostly men, with serious faces and dark clothes (still the culture in North Yorkshire). I had a coughing fit half way through the service. It came from the depths, racking spasms and uncontrollable. The funeral director brought me a glass of water. No good. Oh SOS, what could I do? I then decided boldness was the only way. I held up my hand and excused myself for a moment to sort myself out in the corridor beyond the chapel, but tossing over my shoulder the instruction 'chat amongst yourselves'. How could I ever have done that?! Where did it come from? But they did, all about the deceased. They shared their stories in deep, male rumbles in the opportunity of the moment. Later the widow rang me and said, 'Please don't worry about what happened. Ian would have loved that. We all did. It should be able to happen at all funerals.'

Oh yes, and I hitched a lift in Alb once when my car broke down on the way to a funeral! And I did get there on time!

145

Alb goes to Harvest Festival
'Mother and Baby are Doing Fine' was the caption of a certain photograph taken of me wearing Alb, with my giant pumpkin resting before me on the font, proudly gracing Thormanby's Harvest festival (see the back cover). I had achieved the ambition announced the previous year in my annual letter to distant friends.

Greetings from the land of pumpkin growing competitions! I'm going to grow one too next year. You have to wrap them up at nights, I understand, because THAT IS WHEN THEY GROW! Strangely the pumpkin club is also where I can often network current pastoral information about what is required in terms of hospital admission, etc.

I was started off with a plant grown from seed by the village's expert, 'Pu'rr it in and I'll bring yer the instructions termorrer.' So, I cleared a largish patch (about a metre square) and planted it, only to get the instructions the following day which said that the space needed to grow one pumpkin to a respectable size was actually bigger than my whole garden. Needless to say, I did not win (how could I when some pumpkins arrived at the judging in wheelbarrows, the winner in a trailer?) But I was awarded a 'Commended' for trying!

Alb experiences the Irish Bush Telegraph
We arrived in the little rural Southern Ireland village, beginning to gather as a family for Jeremy and Elaine's wedding. You could tell it was very 'back in time' there, but that was its charm. Tame seals flopped around the car park in the nearby harbour, in contrast with the very prominent wind turbines en route. This was an era when there was much Euro money in Southern Ireland. Elaine's Dad is a retired spud farmer, with a large family of six daughters and a son, and on the way to his home I popped in at the RC church to leave my alb and scarf ready for the next day and to meet the priest, who had kindly invited me to take

part in the leading of the marriage service. What an honour and totally unprecedented and unimagined in those remote Catholic parts!

Some elderly ladies of the parish called in whilst the Father and I were in conversation, the alb over the back of a pew, and BEFORE we had even reached the as yet unvisited new family at home (10-15 minutes later), the word had gone round the WHOLE community that *'There is a woman WITH ROBES in the church talking to Fr M!'*

Alb's own demise

In Holy Week 2011, Alb walked with me and my little congregations as day after day we recalled the steps of Jesus and the walk of his final week. On Monday, the anointing at Bethany; Tuesday, the turning over of the tables in the Temple; Wednesday, Holy Communion; Thursday, the last Supper and washing of feet; then Friday, the scourging, the stripping and the Crucifixion of Jesus. That year I didn't fully experience the joy of the Resurrection on Easter Day, as I had myself decided that this would be the last time I walked that particular walk, accompanied whether by Alb or no. I had made the decision to leave the Church of England.

Brafferton Church

I had been told on my appointment seven years before to 'Go and love the people'. I did. They taught me so much, but at 64, as a woman, lay and non-stipendiary minister, of twenty-five years' affirmed experience, I left with no title, no pension, no tools of the trade, no authority, no licence and finally, 'You are not allowed to wear your robes or look in any way as if you are an Anglican minister still.'... Stripped.

147

The frictions exposed in the dynamics of the pioneering post nearly finished me off but in fact have set me free. I could use lots of holy words of Scripture to reflect this outcome but instead choose to use words from my favourite film of all time, The Exotic Marigold Hotel. The young Indian boy hotel manager who says he has never known any triumphs, only disasters, always responds by saying:
'Everything will be all right in the end and if it isn't all right, then it isn't the end'! I preached offering that hope in a nonconformist church on Easter Day 2012.

I offer a short reflection which you might like to use if you ever have to walk away with sadness... I used it as a part of a liturgy with a small group of trusted friends, in order to be able to lay down with tears the official garments of my Anglican ministry. Thus, I am again free to work alongside those of any faith or no faith at all in love and freedom. Well, in truth I always did, which is why I expect I hit the 'glass ceiling'. Ouch! But it was not easy at my age to step away from the institution and risk being a pioneer again!
Reflection: *Recall the things you have outgrown, left behind, or given up so that you would be able to create the future you envisioned, your personal not-yet. What is it in your imagined future that you can love enough, generatively, that you are willing to do whatever it takes to bring it about?*

Cassock and surplice

******

148

Naked and you called me

Purple
Acts 16: 13-15, Rev.21: 10,22-25, John 14: 23 –29

Whilst thinking about Lydia the purple dye seller about whom I was to preach one Sunday, I was reminded of the poem, 'When I am old I shall Wear Purple'. It's actually called "Warning", which seems appropriate when we are talking about what happens when the Holy Spirit goes to work! I noticed that in 1996 it was voted Britain's favourite poem. Therefore, it must in some mysterious way speak to the very heart of the people we are now, here in our society. Written by Jenny Joseph, it speaks of a longing one day to wear inappropriate clothes; to act in inappropriate ways; to eat inappropriate food. And a regret in still to be conforming for now... though a little surreptitious advance practice might not go amiss?!

This bizarre poem could be a prompting to us in our Christian life that maybe we should again, like the early church, learn to live a little more dangerously. It speaks about something fundamental but largely unacknowledged in most of us. We know in our hearts the changes we would like to make, the changes maybe we should make in order to be more fully alive, but we put it off. This poem encourages us to take risks; to be more outrageous, courageous for what we believe.

So, how do we begin this 'practising'? We mostly come with feeling not good enough, not having the right words, the right skills. Well, here is the promise to help us. It is not we who have to do these things, but we are told the Holy Spirit will teach us everything. How will that happen?

Jesus says, 'I am going away, and I am coming to you.'
How must that bunch of puzzled, anxious men have heard those words of paradox? Jesus deals with them so lovingly. 'And now I have told you this before it occurs, so that when it does occur, you may believe.'

So how do we hear those words for ourselves today? 'I am going away, and I am coming to you.'

The clue to this is in Jesus' previous words. 'My peace I leave with you; my peace I give unto you. Not as the world gives do I give you.' Not a peace of quiet, but ambiguously a peace of empowerment. 'I am going away, and I am coming to you.'

When we compare the experience of the Holy Spirit in the lives of those pioneers of the early church, we see ourselves in a very different situation today. People are not now hearing the Good News for the first time. We are alongside a generation that has heard it and largely rejected it, and then even more sadly a next generation who by and large are given little or no opportunity now to hear it at all. It is easy to become discouraged. And we may ask, 'How might we begin to recover the image of God in which we were made? And thus,

149

then more effectively help others to meet him too.' Yet those early Christians were just the ordinary people of their time. An Old Testament passage describes the dream of a wild Old Testament prophet, Ezekiel, about all the dry bones in a burial valley, joining up and coming together clothed in sinew and flesh. And God's glorious promise. 'I will put a new spirit within you. You will be my people and I will be your God.'

What are the dry bones in my life, now at this moment, which need knitting together?' What needs to be reborn, made whole, rekindled, reordered into a new energy in my life?

These early disciples, a humble band of fearful men, in the empowerment of the Holy Spirit, went out, and their faith eventually converted the Roman Empire and changed history. Is it now a different Holy Spirit, or a spent and exhausted Holy Spirit? Is that why our churches are declining? Or maybe we are not sure what our role is any longer? Thankfully, the responsibility is not ours to convert people. That is God's work. It is not within our gift to do that. But the power of God has to reach others through us. The Gospel is not about success, but about faithfulness. And it is our responsibility to continue to listen with an open heart and to be ready to respond. Look what we read about Lydia's conversion, 'The Lord opened her heart to listen eagerly'. It was the Lord who opened her heart. But then she responds, 'Come and stay at my home.' She begins to step out and explore further immediately. Jesus affirms this hospitality by promising, 'My father and I will make our home with those who love me.'

God is now present in a new and unique way. King he still is, but one who makes his home within our hearts; living within and alongside us, with this peace which will hold us, love us into new life and sustain us through the storm: it challenges and empowers us to step out in faith and courage.

Is Jesus Christ today calling us to be a little more outrageous and courageous in his name? Are we ready to start practising to more fully enter that empowering peace of God, as we are called to renewal of his church? We can start so simply by just listening anew to the whisper of God in the most unlikely places. Because to listen is to give true hospitality to another.

Jesus said, 'I have told you this before it occurs, so that when it does occur, you will believe it.' Ezekiel dreamed of a great sound of the rattling of bones as they came together. One heck of a racket. So don't be alarmed, because change does not necessarily happen silently or unnoticed. That is the joy and sometimes the pain of it. God says, 'I will put my spirit within you and you will live. You will know when I have done it.'

When you are old, will you wear purple? You could tell your family and friends before you begin, so that when it does occur they will have been warned!

Jane, Ann and Sue - three sisters, now rather more individualistic!

**

This reflective section concludes with a difficult and painful issue which may well resonate, especially with women, who have metaphorically dared to 'wear purple' or left the red shoes on for too long in a pioneering or risky situation...

******

The Scapegoat
Acts 16: 16-34. John 17: 20-26

Sometimes, in my mind, I like to alter the names of the well-known stories of the Bible. E.g. I might re-name the 'Parable of the Lost Sheep', that of the 'Diligent Shepherd'. The 'Prodigal Son', the 'Loving Father' or even the ' Absent Mother'. The 'Good Samaritan' becomes the 'Rule bound Holy Men' or 'Compassion for a Stranger'. And maybe the 'Parable of the Sower' is 'How is the condition of my own soil?'

This is not such a frivolous and cranky exercise as it may initially seem. For me, it gives added insight. It promotes my own deeper reflection, and it enriches for me the Word of God; building on how I can better hear Him speaking to me today through these old and well-loved stories, right into the heart of my own situation.

So then, this astonishing account from Acts. It is a story so rich in the miraculous, the heroic, the courageous and yet also, a warning! I love Acts. It's full of ordinary people filled by the grace of God; empowered by the Holy Spirit. Here is the account of a young, vigorous church, full of joy and enthusiasm, but also it is a book encountering human, fallible people. Peter, who is totally aston-

151

ished when he finds himself miraculously freed from prison. The man who fell asleep during a sermon, tumbling out of a window. Lydia the dealer in purple cloth; a woman, the first recorded Christian convert in Europe, all here in a rich tapestry of life.

So, what would you say that this story has been about? How has it spoken to you for yourself? Yes. This a story of the miraculous; God looking after the faithful; His own.

We read, 'About midnight Paul and Silas were singing hymns and praying to God and the prisoners were listening to them. Suddenly there was an earthquake so violent that the foundations of the prison were shaken; and immediately all the doors were opened and everyone's chains were unfastened'. And yes. This was a story of courageous missionaries suffering profoundly for the sake of the Gospel. 'The crowd joined in attacking them, and the magistrates stripped them of their clothing and ordered them to be beaten with rods. After they had given them a severe flogging they threw them into prison and fastened their feet into stocks'.

Also, we heard they were men of integrity. They did not run away and thereby get the jailer into a difficulty which would have cost him his life. Paul shouted to reassure him, "Do not harm yourself, for we are still here."

It is a story about the actual saving of the jailer's life. When the jailer woke up and saw the prison doors all open, he drew his sword to kill himself'. It was a saving not only of his earthly life but of his life for eternity. He and his entire family were baptized without delay.'

Or we could call it the story of the unscrupulous slave-owners. And then note how the Baddies were confounded at the last as Paul and Silas walked free.

I tell you; there were pages and pages in my commentaries about all these stories. The story of the miraculous God. The courageous missionaries of integrity. The redemption and rejoicing of the jailor and his family. The story of the unscrupulous and money-grabbing slave-owners and the slave girl's fortune telling and prophesy. And yes. We can learn from these incidents again and again that He is a God of miracles. We do need to stay focused in Him and not become distracted by the false gods of our own age. It is worth pausing a moment and wondering just what they might be. We do need to take risks and if necessary suffer for the sake of the gospel truths. We are to rejoice with others for their salvation and redemption and learn from the foiling of the dastardly plans of the unscrupulous.

But, wait. There was nothing at all in any of my large and erudite tomes about it being a story of silence. The silence of what happened to the slave girl who ceased to be a source of income for those who had exploited her. While she followed Paul she would cry out, 'These men are slaves of the most high God'. She kept doing this for many days. And Paul, very much annoyed, turned and said to the spirit, 'I order you in the name of Jesus Christ to come out of her.' And it came out that very hour. And when her owners saw that their hope of making money was gone, they seized Paul and Silas and dragged them into the market place before the authorities. If that's what they did to Paul and Silas, I wonder what they did to her. What do you suppose happened to her after she had been healed and silenced so that her owners could no longer use her? Did Paul give her another thought, I wonder, whilst he was singing hymns and praising God to the other prisoners in jail?

The story of the silencing of the slave girl. It's easy to forget and lose sight of the scapegoat? Maybe this can be a reminder to us that in our zeal we can be in danger of striding on in confidence that we have got it right, indeed often for the best of all possible motives, whilst someone or some others are falling through the net.

Maybe we have ourselves known what it is to have been that person; invisible, dispensable, an 'embarrassment', speaking out with a truth no one wants to hear; being the voice which really needs to be heard. We shall never know what happened to that girl who was no longer of any use to those who had abused her. We can only speculate. But it seems unlikely that she ever walked free.

Whose is the voice in this story that you and I need to hear today? It will probably be different for each of us. That is the infinite gift of God's word.
Is it that of Paul and Silas with their courage and heroism for the sake of the gospel?
Is it that of the miraculous God manifest all around us?
Is it the voice of the jailer in his joy of redemption and salvation?
Is it the voice of law and order of the authorities?
Or is it the voice of the silent?
The voice of the silence of the forgotten; the abused; the powerless; the dispensable?

Through them all, if we are listening, it is for sure that we will hear the voice of Jesus Christ, the scapegoat for us all. Hear His voice as He prepares to die. The voice of compassion and hope for us all, even in his own fear, as He prays to His Father:
'I ask not only on behalf of these, but also on behalf of those, that the love with which you have loved me may be in them, and I in them. And that the world may know you have sent me and have loved them, even as you have loved me.'

Jesus says for us now too, 'I ask not only on behalf of these, but also on behalf of those still wandering in the wilderness.'

******

Scape-Coat. Rending the clothes

Biblical Jewish tradition of Scapegoat:
Job 1: 20

Early Israelites devised this method for advertising grief and shame. It involved a man publicly wrapping his body in sackcloth and strewing his hair

153

with ashes. The rough goat's hair cloth, with distinctive smell, irritated the skin and dirty ashes became a physical manifestation of his distressed state. The outward clothing of an inward grief, a coded communication.

An actual goat came to symbolise this on behalf of the masses and would eventually be sent out in to the desert to die. So the word, scapegoat, has come to mean a person who is blamed and punished for the sins, crimes or sufferings of others, with the consequence of generally distracting attention from the real perpetrators of the injustice!

In modern usage, a scapegoat may be a child, employee, peer, ethnic or religious group singled out for unmerited negative treatment or blame. A whipping boy or fall guy is a form of scapegoat.

Gethsemane Garments Exhibition, 2010

Revd Peter Privett, the creator and designer of the four Gethsemane garments, leaves us with an enduring challenge. In particular the Scapegoat garment in sackcloth, which comprises ripped linen, cotton, muslin, dyed and painted beads, bones, shells and cotton and wool threads. It reveals the feelings and emotions of the suffering, being made from ripped strips of material, ie life is shredded.

The Scapegoat (Leviticus 16: 20-26, clothed with ashes,) has always been a desperately sad and poignant image for me ever since studying the haunting painting by Holman Hunt of that name. Years later I read an inspirational book called Women Who Run with the Wolves by Clarissa Pinkola Estees. In one of the chapters, she recognises that many women have found themselves scapegoated; maybe even several times in their lives, such that it becomes an unhealthy pattern of wilderness wandering. She suggests that self-awareness is key and offers a creative way of recognizing and processing that life-denying burden of shame and ashes. With somewhat 'black humour', she suggests we make ourselves a Scape-Coat. She suggested using a real old garment of our own, with significantly placed patches, but I have chosen another version of working with this creative image. Recently on my Personal and Spiritual Development course we were encouraged to write an angry psalm. I chose one of the angrier ones of King David on which to pray and reflect, and subsequently dared to write my own.

So, I offer what emerged from this reflection, an 'angry' psalm as my personal 'Scape-Coat'. It helped me to move through a very painful time in my life. Even more significantly in having been given 'permission' to do it, it has become liberating and life giving.

Passionate God, why have you allowed this to happen to me again?
You call me to a place to 'Go and love the people'.
I am obedient to your call and work tirelessly, generously and joyfully.
But then, you send another one who cannot sustain the work.
I am now exhausted, fearful,

154

In yet another landscape, without a map.
Even if I had one I couldn't read it.
I cannot respect any who bully me.
I cannot respect one who acts as Pontius Pilate.

I am alone and sinking.
My gut burns and rages within me.
Crumble away my enemies,
Make mincemeat of those who are jealous and feel threatened!

And yet my own sin and part in this I offer to you in supplication for your mercy?
Come and reign again in the temple of my heart.
Show me how I must change, so that as in the falling of the dew in the morning,
I can be refreshed.
You knew me through and through before I was made in my mother's womb.
You know that authority always could be a problem for me.

Show me a new path, O Navigator God.
Walk with me as I stumble and fall.
Hold my hand and lead me in my blindness.
In my reluctance, urge me on.
In my complacency, challenge me.
In my fear, help me to trust again.
In my hunger for acceptance, feed me.
In my burning pain, cool me.
In my pride, gentle me with humility
And for my breaking heart, hold me and never let me go.

Yet, even though I remain unheard,
And the ashes of the scapegoat
Are once again heaped upon me:
though I am weary in my bones,
and my spirit sorely aches within me:
Even so will I continue to serve you;
Even so will I worship you, always.
And never will I cease to share your faithful,
Gracious, astonishing love with those whom I am called to serve.
Thus will I sing continually your everlasting song of praise,
For ever, and forevermore.
Amen

'Beware, the scapegoats are returning from the wilderness!' ...

******

...in a purple cloak, on a more joyful occasion outdoors

Chapter 7

Last scene of all that ends this strange eventful history...sans everything? Not yet! Now with another satchel, this time a yellow one!

Wearing Out

2011 until Today

In which I retired?... moved to live in a remote farmhouse... became more in-volved with assorted generations... worked part time again.

The Seventh Age

Naked and you clothed me
i)   What do I wear in my retirement?
ii)   Black and white for Choir
iii)   Lost Cycle Specs
iv)   Yves St Laurent
v)   No Room at the Inn
vi)   Chatelaine
vii)   Leaving them behind
viii)   To Scatter or not to Scatter? That is the Question!
ix)   Continuing to Age and Reflect
x)   Enter Stage Eight…Amazed by Joy!
xi)   Aging as a Married Woman, in the Third Millennium after Seven Decades

Naked and you called me
xii)   Grave Clothes, Shrouds
xiii)   The Madonna of the Cross
xiv)   Clothing. Be dressed and ready for Service!

Naked and you clothed me

What do I wear in my retirement?

My long fluffy cardi, pale blue, soft mohair, hand knitted and silk lined which Paul found when we were packing to leave my ministry house. He had bought it for me from a craft fair years ago and secreted it in the garage for one day to bring out as a surprise! It was a surprise, and most surprising was firstly that he was himself surprised to rediscover it, and secondly that it was complete and whole and not at all eaten or nested in by mice! It is the lightest and yet warmest garment I have ever possessed. I wear it as a dressing gown; for swimming trips; for best over my navy and white striped pirate trousers, and with my short denim skirt. It packs away into a tiny space in suitcase or my tardis bag. It is a coat for cool evenings when I go to see Emma in Riparbella. It shortly had to have a new adventure of a more intrepid and scary nature. It came with me to hospital for a fairly major operation, so was a good and cosy companion there as a bed jacket.

I still have to wear the right clothes for professional occasions, for example when I take funeral services for those who do not wish me to wear any church paraphernalia. This is where Wall's sale catalogue comes into its own. (Here I am in good company as Diana Athill says the same.) Their clothes are innovative in design and interesting in shape, with irregular hem lines and glorious fabrics and colours. But definitely smart and respectful! For such occasions, I often wear a simple dark grey heavy ribbed cotton midcalf length dress with long sleeves. It is almost impossible to describe because of its shape around the hem and in how it is caught up towards the side, yet it hangs fitting closely, formally and elegantly. I have two current Wall favourites; one a crushed raspberry soft silky velvet dress, knee length, long sleeves. Although feeling exotic to wear, it is actually very simple and understated, but can be dressed up with scarf, co-ordinating tights, and of course jewellery. I have even teamed it up on occasion with my 'Goth' red lined, designer, multi-laced ankle boots, which were acquired from a charity shop where they had long languished as being too small for most people to wear! I am also enjoying an oversized shirt, which can be worn as shirt or jacket. This garment, with a mandarin collar set off by my Grandma's rose gold brooch, is also soft silky velvet, with vibrant deep autumnal colours on a background of the deepest olive green which can almost appear to be black in some lights.

My favourite comfortable wear for home and away, however, are my various baggy trousers. They might have come from Toast and be blue and white stripes, or brought back from Goa for me by my friend who winters there every year. Emma sends me hand-made leather Moroccan shoes now and again which team up nicely. Not terribly practical for my occasional dog-walking, I acknowledge. I have an extra pair of pirate trousers currently because my friend has made me a second pair out of a long navy and white striped skirt! A sequel to this is that the teenage daughter of a friend was so enamoured of the first tatty pair with a large hole in the knee, that she is now the proud possessor of same! I understand that she wears them to her Quaker school on 'no uniform' days.

My greatest clothes discovery thus far at the end of my seventh decade leapt off a desk at me in a vintage clothes shop in St. Ives. I had gone with my sartorially motivated friend to Cornwall to help her look after her son's pair of bulldogs whilst he was abroad. One of the great joys of that week for me was to hop on a bus each afternoon for Evensong at Truro Cathedral. One evening they were singing the Stanford in B Magnificat and Nunc Dimittis, and the numinous atmosphere even in that beautiful building was elevated by several notches. I was in tears and the man sitting next to me likewise. After the service I asked him, 'Was one of those your boy?' He was still visibly moved and replied, 'They are all my boys. I am the headmaster!'

I have digressed. In that vintage clothes shop I discovered one of the answers to my 'what should I now wear for my professional ministry occasions?' There it was, languishing on the desk, not even having reached the hanging rail stage, but as I met it eye to eye, we recognised each other immediately. It is long, plain black silk velvet, lined with hand painted silk, black and white, which is designed to just peek out in a waterfall from the collar and reveres. It has what is known as a handkerchief hem and throws on over anything and transforms it. It has already had a sad accident, however, as its lovely pointy hem became caught in the wheel of the wheelchair which took me into hospital from the ambulance to A and E, on morphine in huge pain and pretty much out of it. A sign of my times, I suppose. I have as invisibly as I possibly can repaired it, and its life will continue, a bit battered and damaged but fixed well enough to still play its part. It is no longer perfect but that is just like its new owner too, I admit.

There is another coat which is special for me, and I was reminded of why that was in the Woman's Hour programme 'We are what we wear.' It was Charlotte who spoke of a 'watery' dress and that to put it on was like entering water. 'Myself,' she said. Magical outside and inside.

I feel the metamorphosis similarly in my ankle-length, teal velvet 'Chrissie' coat. The material subtly shimmers in rivulets, as I move. One night I was wearing it in an extraordinary 'religious context', where an extremely exotic-looking lady approached me and said quietly in my ear, 'I covet that coat immediately'!

Everything for travel fits into my tardis bag, named after Dr Who's telephone box, whose space inside is infinite. It is a sort of zipped linen bag/holdall. The linen fabric has a Liberty print of William Morris design and is very light, which is a huge bonus, both for carrying about and especially when travelling by air, with all those significant weight ramifications. Amazingly it stays clean over the years, having been on airport floors, railway station platforms, trains, car boots, etc. It goes on retreat, holiday, family visits, abroad, weekend jaunts and to the grandchildren in London, Bedfordshire and Cambridgeshire. Its long handles mean it can be worn over a shoulder, so it is easy to cart about. It didn't go to hospital with me though, in case it got lost! Neither did my yellow satchel (bought for me by my sister from the Shambles in York) accompany me, for the same reason.

**

I still occasionally get to sing in a choir in my retirement; along with the usual 'what shall I wear conundrum', as you will see...

******

Black and White for Choir
Written in 2015

      I love being in this choir which meets twice a year for Easter and Advent, though Peter the choir master never knows who will turn up to sing from churches in the Deanery or beyond.

      Today was the final rehearsal for the Deanery Advent service. The church with candles (a special sacred liturgical component of this service) is being prepared. Brasses are polished, buffed and shone; refreshments (no wine in this church, only tea or coffee) being prepared and put out at the end of the Nave; the music has been practised, honed and refined for weeks. This is the service of the church year where we begin to turn our hearts, minds and souls both to the coming of the baby Jesus Christ, and also in tradition to the Second Coming of the Messiah at some future unspecified date. It heralds a time of stillness and reflection and a calling to repentance and examination of the health of our souls contrasting with our frantic secular preparations for Christmas festivities and our seductive summons to the temples of shopping malls and internet sites.

      Our singing under an experienced, patient and gentle choir master is as ready as it could be, given the arbitrary collection of singers, as we gather to lead worship for the Deanery on the night of all nights. This atmospheric service is rich in numinous all round, as it opens in total darkness with the unaccompanied choir singing from the end of the Nave that spine-tingling Advent Matins' Responsory 'I looked from afar', composed by 16th C. Palestrina.

      It is 4.15. We fold up our music and place it in order for later, pencils on the sill of the pew in the choir stall in front, just in case of last minute necessary changes, and we are bidden to return half an hour before the scheduled service. There is just time to go home, have our tea and be back by 6.00pm. *'Dress, black and white of course for ladies and men in dark suits with shirt and tie.'* My heart sank. I had overlooked this requirement in all the excitement of being able to sing in this choir again. 'H'm!' I reflect, 'not long.'

      I approached my wardrobe in trepidation; half an hour to find something acceptable. I fumbled around on the back hooks for my long black silky

161

Indian skirt. Phew! There it was, tucked under a white blouse. Oh no, short sleeves. Heart begins to thump. Garments strewn across the bedroom now (sort it out later) – oh, here is another old white blouse; skirt on, blouse on: oh dear, bigger bosoms now. Buttons are straining fit to 'bust'. No. NO.

I know, white T-shirt with long sleeves. I can wear my white silk scarf cleverly arranged around my neck. Now scarves whirl dervishly out of the scarf drawer, and no, the white silky one had vanished. Ten minutes to go. A white shirt of my husband's maybe? Absolutely not! It would not go with the soft, feminine silky skirt. I am even now, dare I admit the subversive nature of the thought, flirting with the idea of hauling out the blast from the past cassock and surplice. Oh NO! That thought must be banished back to the Reptile Brain, where it belongs!

I'll just go and polish my black shoes whilst I wait for the muse to strike and there in the kitchen I saw the solution. It jumped out at me from a large terracotta Grecian urn, sidling up to the Aga.

I left on time in polished black high heels, black tights, black mini skirt, black polo neck jumper. Natty little black velvet Laura Ashley jacket with stand-up collar, attached to which, affixed with a large safety pin (which I had failed to put away earlier in the week, so I knew where it was), a life size white silk hydrangea flower head.

Black and white. I had done it. A bit outrageous, and a daunting prospect, in the same church where it had been implied that I would never be ordained because I wore the wrong sort of clothes.

But Oh bliss Oh joy, I bumped into the ever gracious choir master on the way in, who let me past!

So, yes, I could sing the Palestrina and Bach's 'Wake oh Wake' and all the other glorious Advent music after all.

The next year...guess what. Two or three of the other ladies were in all black with jaunty flowers affixed.

**

And talking of possibly outrageous little accessories...

******

Lost Cycle Specs!
Written in 2014

Paul and I on a leisurely ramble in Oxford one day went into the enticing vintage clothes shop at the junction near Magdalen College of the Iffley and Cowley Roads.

I am not good at conventional retail spending, but on this occasion I could not resist this outrageous nonsense of a purchase. They were large white bicycle sun specs with wheel rims, spokes on the lenses; a saddle springing from the left eye frame crossing the bar to handle bars and red handle grips from the left. Oh, they were wonderfully eccentric and for a fiver I could not leave them languishing in that shop. There will never be an occasion to wear them, I thought, but I could have them on the mantelpiece. No wonder my mother used to despair of me.

But then...

Oh my goodness, the Tour de France came to Yorkshire, and all along the route we pulled out all the stops for a welcome in true Yorkshire hospitality style. Painted yellow bicycles hung from walls and were propped up alongside fences, walls and chained to posts for months. Spectators queued long and deep on the day to cheer the cyclists on. The Tour de France director said that Yorkshire's welcome was the best he had experienced, whilst these parts just said, 'granc

Not the Tour de France bike!

163

This was the moment for the cycle specs quite obviously, especially as the little girl twins of our neighbours would be in that throng. Yes, they should have them. I think all of the party enjoyed them to their maximum but sadly they never returned safely. Later I found a picture of the very same specs in the Express. 'Were they mine?' I mutter darkly to myself. However, c'est la vie. My specs did have the most exciting and most memorable and unique of all possible outings!

**

So next from the ridiculous to the sublime...

******

Yves St Laurent

In November 2015, I was privileged to journey twice to the Bowes Museum in Northumberland where there was a unique opportunity to enter a breath-taking exhibition of original clothing garments and designs by Yves St Laurent – the first exhibition of his work in the United Kingdom. I am inspired by his approach to a new creation with a blank canvas in the spirit of, "I try to forget all I have learned". "The very act of drawing creates the design. When I hold a pencil, I don't know what I am going to draw. The garments evolve; almost draw themselves once I have the face of the woman I am dressing."

The arena is light dimmed, in deference to the age and preciousness of these exquisite fabrics. This exhibition is nothing to do with 'fashion'. Yves St Laurent writes, "Fashion fades. Style is eternal". As we enter, before us is a catwalk video, recording the modelling of all the awesome garments we are shortly to gaze upon, displayed for real as we wander around the room. It is no longer just a 'room', more like a 'Cathedral'.

We learn that he crafted his garments around how women worked, lived and moved, which above all focused on their role and activity in society rather than putting fashion first. Thus, he is described as a socially conscious designer. He is the first to use elements of the male wardrobe, for example the trouser suit, to be worn in a completely feminine way and he viewed the ambiguity this provoked as defining the modern woman of his time, giving women confidence, audacity and powers whilst preserving their femininity.

He reflected, with widespread appeal, the art typical of the 60s pop culture – democratising the high art usually only found in museums (e.g. the Picasso squarey one). In this innovative way a woman embodied a painting in the form of a garment. I sense an unusual ambiguity of realistic humility and arrogance in his gift – he would say, "The most beautiful clothes that can dress a woman are the arms of the man she loves. If she does not have that, I am there."

164

A particularly startling and enigmatic section arose from YSL's belief that "A woman's most beautiful garment is her nakedness", describing his experimenting with transparency, veiling the body "like a hymn to the beauty of nudity", thereby creating the paradox of a dress that completely covered the body whilst highlighting its nudity! Hide and seek adding to the feminine aura of sensuality!

Increasingly I was being affirmed in my dawning realisation that clothes do indeed have a spiritual significance. YSL writes, 'Elegance is a way of life; a way of moving through the world' and he asks, "Isn't elegance about completely forgetting what one is wearing?" The introduction to the Bowes Museum Exhibition indeed begins with a spiritual connotation. "He very much believed that a woman should be free to express who she really is through her attire". This is developed with other 'spiritual language'.

The word 'homage' is used again and again when referring to YSL's tribute to the contribution of painters and artists to his designs and ultimately garments. While seeking to design for the present, he also paid homage to his favourite artists and used the sumptuous exuberance that haute couture offers to express his simultaneous nostalgia for the past.

Garments are specifically described in the exhibition as:

i)   Homage to Pablo Picasso. Black and red 'point d'esprit' net blouse; loose fitting harlequin patchwork skirt of pink satin, faille and velvet.

ii)   Homage to William Shakespeare. Wedding gown of puckered golden silk damask double coat with coral coloured lining; golden silk damask wedding gown with golden embroidery.

iii)   Homage to Vincent van Gough. White evening jacket in silk organza embroidered with an iris motif composed of sequins, bugle beads, seed beads and ribbons in shades of blue, purple, green and orange jewelled buttons.

Cocktail dress

165

Others include 'homage' to Henri Matisse, George Braque, playwright Jean Cocteau and poet Louis Aragon.

And in a category of its own was the stunning Peace Cape. Here is its description: Yellow silk satin cape embroidered with a sun surrounded by two doves; embroidery composed of yellow, pink and fuchsia sequins, yellow, fuscia and black bugle beads...

It was an indescribable experience in that place on that day, and it is impossible to convey here the awe and wonder (more spiritual terms) that it evoked in my heart and yes, spirit. As with spiritual and sacred experiences, I can return to it in my imagination and memory and it can still be as real and as life enhancing as it was then.

So along with all the awesome spirituality word parallels, 'homage', 'Miracle of the moment', 'style is eternal'. 'A hymn to the beauty of nudity'. I was 'inspired' in that word's original sense of an 'inbreathing of spirit'. I hope this does not seem heretical, but it cannot be denied that vision may pass from soul to soul. From the creator comes the gift of art – intuited by the designer, interpreted by the crafter and ultimately producing a garment which inspires a relationship both with its wearer and an onlooker who can thus share in the glory of God as being fully alive!

**

And so now back to the reality of everyday...

******

No Room at the Inn
Written in 2014

I recall a significant film shot of John Cleese. He is stuck in mud alongside his elderly and by now terminally exhausted car in the middle of a field, already late for a crucial engagement. Legs akimbo and pacing furiously, his hand is clapped to his forehead. In dire distress, he shakes his other fist and wails at the stress of frustrated intent and emotions, 'It isn't the despair, it is the hope!' And yes, sometimes the 'hope' can feel more anguished, fragile and tenuous than the 'despair'. Dare we trust in the hope?

For the past five years, I have cared for my mother for a week in the summer, whilst my father set off intrepidly on the train alone, taking a ferry to meet an old shipmate in France as part of a Normandy Veteran group.
HOPE...

This year was special for my father, because it was the final official gathering in Normandy, this time with heads of states present to honour all who died and those who survived that attack. He knew he was to be awarded the medal of the Légion d'Honneur. All year he had anticipated this occasion in hope. At 91, he is my mother's fulltime carer (24 hours a day, 7 days a week) as she has slipped into early vascular dementia. This year, however, neither of my sisters nor I felt able to care for our mother safely at her home, whilst he had this break. Thus gently over the last few months we have tried to help her to accept a respite care home for a week. All was ready; clothes packed and name taped. Sewing on all those tapes to my mum's clothes reminded me of how many she must have sewn for four of us onto so many items of school uniform over the years. I was to stay in their bungalow and visit her whilst Dad was away, but two nights before she was due to go the home phoned my father to say there was now no room for her there, as the lift had broken and her allocated room was upstairs. They had found her a place in another care home. She absolutely refused to go there!

Devon village signs

DESPAIR...

At 5.00pm he rang me in despair. 'What am I going to do? I have to have this break.'

HOPE...

9.00am the next day, I rang in fear and trepidation, because the consequences of this conversation going awry at this stage of events were some-

167

what unthinkable, and I am embarrassed and confused to report that an occupant of a downstairs room had died in the night. She could now go after all!

I left Yorkshire and travelled the four hours to my parents' bungalow and took her into the respite centre fifteen miles away. My father opted to remain at home, probably quite wisely. Exhausted, I settled into bed for an early night.

DESPAIR...

8.30pm, the night staff rang to say they couldn't cope with my mother, could I help? She was determined to come home. I was angry. My father was also angry and panicking and pacing about and suggesting we get my brother to 'go and sort it out'. That made me even more angry so, virtually incandescent by this time, I dressed and drove hazardously the fifteen miles through the late evening, wondering what on earth I was going to say, do? 'God grant me some wisdom here.'

I arrived in fear and trepidation and somehow heard myself refuse to take her home. My mother was astonished. I told her I was not going home either; that I had to stay in a hotel in the town as I was not driving all those miles all night up and down the road. She was deeply shocked. To stay in a hotel to her was an outrage of unacceptable extravagance...unthinkable. Somehow, this really impacted on her. I offered a choice, 'Mum, I am not going home tonight, so you can choose to stay here or come with me into a hotel.' 'I am staying here then,' she said. I waited until she was settled in bed and set out to find myself a bed for me for the night. The care home knew I was nearby and my Mum knew I would be back in the morning.

HOPE...

Off I went round the town. Bed and Breakfasts, hotels...all full. Finally, as darkness settled, I entered a pub of the darts and snooker variety. 'Well,' said the young barmaid, 'I am sorry, I have no beds, but we have got some pods, sort of shepherd's huts round the back!' At which point the salvation of my black humour kicked in. Hm. Next year's Christmas sermon here! Pods? Shepherd's huts? (My father's description was 'dog kennel', when he saw the photograph.) So, round the back I went. They were situated in a yard adjoining the market, and mercifully next day was not the morning for the trading of beasts of the field. I was given a key for the hut and one for a loo. The landlord blew up a double mattress for me, with his own lungs as his pump battery had expired. And he found a spare duvet in which to wind myself, still in my daytime clothes, for the night. Thank you God, the landlord and the barmaid! Following a rather uncomfortable, sleepless night, I was ashamed I had been so firm with my mother. What if the shock had killed her? What if my Dad had died in the night from anxiety?

168

Tentatively, I re-entered the home in the early morning and the staff smilingly remarked, 'Well we don't know what you said or did with your mother but she is a different woman this morning.'

That week she went from strength to strength. We all began to see a woman we hadn't seen for years. Lively, engaged, initiating conversations, walking, joining in. Dare we trust in the hope? It is fragile and tenuous. How long will this stage last? We get it wrong from time to time, and yet, then comes the grace, gently and lovingly. It has been a privilege to be alongside my lovely intelligent, feisty mother last week; to watch her begin to blossom and grow again, and to spend rare quality time with her at this stage of our lives.

This article first appeared in 'Plus', a quarterly publication by Christians on Ageing.

**

In 2015 my Mum sadly died, but I have one special item of her garments that symbolises her domestic mastery (or mistressy!)...

******

Chatelaine
Written in 2015

1. The mistress of a large house. 2. A set of short chains attached to a woman's belt, for carrying keys etc. Based on medieval Latin, castellamus - 'lord of a castle'.

If you are a period drama viewer, have you ever noticed the chatelaine suspended from the belt of the housekeeper? It is something that reflects who they are – their skills – their authority – their being responsible for the fine tuning of the order of the household. A trust has been placed in their abilities and their integrity.

My father bought one for my mother once, which was hooked over a nail and set against red velvet in a glass fronted box to hang on a wall in the entrance hall. It comprises a pair of small scissors in a beautiful tiny sheath, an exquisitely engraved thimble and a rubber encased in silver. When my Mum died, nothing of hers had been especially bequeathed to me, so I dared to ask my Dad if I could have the chatelaine. He liked the idea of my inheriting it. 'I will bring it at Christmas,' he said. He laughed when I told him I would certainly wear it, not just hang it on a wall. I promised I would use it, treasure it and become a good steward of it. It duly arrived into my safe keeping!

I asked my landlord Chris (expert family jeweller) if he would look at it to determine of which metal it was made, and for me to ask could I, should I, clean it, if so what with? So, on the way out to church one Sunday morning I met him in the yard. Our grownup children were packing their cars ready to return to the South, so in a flurry of activity and 'goodbyes' I handed the chatelaine to Chris, who admired it vastly, never having seen one before, and responded, 'Ideal. I will see my father today and ask his advice.'

I basked complacently in a day of thanksgiving and feeling greatly blessed before departing to lead Evensong in a local parish church. I needed to be slightly intrepid on that occasion in order to negotiate the floods which had brought North Yorkshire to a state of the ark that year. Exhausted, I returned home. Paul was in bed asleep, also exhausted, in the middle of his course of radiotherapy treatment. So, I sat to relax and unwind with a large glass of dry white and the glorious Endeavour TV programme. At 9.45 there was a great and panicky hammering on the door, simultaneously with a phone call from my land-lord. I rushed to the door, there to discover Chris, all white and shaking in his pyjamas and dressing gown. (An outward reflection of his inward state of mind?) 'Have you got it?' he cried. 'Where is it? I thought it would be here by the door.' Then, more or less incoherent now – 'I left it on the roof of Jeremy's car while I fed the dogs and then forgot about it until I have just seen one on The Antiques Road Show and remembered. I can't sleep. Jeremy must have driven off with it on the roof. Which way did he go home? I have been down the drive to look both ways and searched as far as I can.' (Pitch black, drive and lane one mile long in each direction).

Oh my goodness. This was a complete disaster for me too. a) I had been a poor steward of my family's inheritance. b) How on earth am I going to tell Dad? c) Jane should of course have had it. She would have kept it safely.

But mercifully, overriding all this, I felt such compassion towards this lovely, responsible, caring young man. He reminded me of one of my sons, so sorry and so distraught at his momentary carelessness. 'Look Chris, we can't do anything about it now in the dark. Let's revisit it in the morning. Do sleep. It is only a thing.' (Thinking, you haven't run over one of my grandchildren.)

Off I went to bed, thoroughly confounded at this turn of events, texting Jeremy before I could sleep. 'Disaster,' I announced. His reply...?
'Oh, I wondered what that was when I unpacked the car on our return home. Elaine saw it on the car roof, thought it was something of your Mum's to pack for her, so now it's up on our wall.'

Both Chris and I slept soundly that night. I told my dad the story and, bless him, he also said, 'It is only a thing.' Such a moving and gracious response, as he had just so recently been bereaved of my Mum, his wife of seventy years.

I learned later from Chris's wife that it was all equally poignant for him. On that very day, he had been helping his father sort out his deceased mother's clothes. So, I am indeed heartily glad I was able to be gentle with him!

**

And as the older generation begins to depart, how does the next generation begin to process the aftermath?...

******

Leaving them Behind

2015 was our Annus Horribilis or, if one is not the Queen, a 'b***** of a year!'

It was the year both Paul's father and my mother died, both of whose funerals I have had the privilege of conducting. Paul's Mum took off to North Cyprus two weeks after the funeral of Alan, and she is intending never to return, even to keep her NHS stuff going. (She can buy all her existing medication cheaper there from a shop anyway.) Paul's brother Keith and his wife have already retired there. She is now living the dream at over 90 and good luck to her! Where are her 32 bikinis? ('I only really need the bottoms here Jackie, where are they?') But at least I discovered her final resting place clothing request for when the time comes. *'I want to be buried in my orange sandals, orange scarf and gold Chinese dress. Everyone is to wear bright colours, because that is how I have lived my life.'* I had a phone call from her recently to tell me she had at last been able to find somewhere there where she could buy some more clothes. *'Wonderful. I have bought 15 new pairs of shorts and 5 T–shirts so far!'*

Since then we have been out to see her and she has taken North Cyprus by storm, eating out in beach bars many evenings, joined a club, learned to use the i-Pad to connect with relatives all over the world. She goes regularly to market, auctions and parties, sometimes up until midnight.

I have asked Jackie, Paul's sister, to share some of her mother's clothes story as Kathleen did encapsulate the legend that some women accu-

171

mulate and hoard clothes to an extraordinary degree. She is also proud that she took 'matching' likewise. Everything in her clothing every day is put on from the lowliest of her undergarments to coordinate with everything which goes over them. Kathleen explained to me once that this was also in case she had an accident and was taken into hospital.

So, Jackie writes:

Decisions, decisions, choices, choices; I could do with a diagram/picture of a brain in overload here, as I approach with trepidation this task in a four-bed-roomed house, with twelve wardrobes, numerous drawers, shelves in cupboards, under the bed storage, a loft with suitcases bursting at the seams, a conservatory, a garage, not to mention two sheds. This sorting out was a very daunting prospect; a mammoth task, a lifetime of memories and treasures. Some things she wanted to take to Cyprus. What to leave behind?

They were Mum's things, not mine or yours, my lovely, lovely Mum's treasured possessions, of she who brought me up to look after things properly, carefully. They cost money which had been hard saved for; sometimes expensive items, sometimes cheap or bargains in sales; well some were, some weren't the bargain we thought! They would then have had to be returned, exchanged or even altered to fit - yet more money, but cherished, worn and loved nevertheless, and now here came the crunch.

If you have had to do this for a parent, you are probably aware of the piles which have to be made: to 'throw away', to 'go to charity', 'to keep' and 'don't know'. This last pile is the tricky one to be looked at again later in more detail. Maybe these clothes can be altered again to fit, make more fashionable, or maybe there would be no room for them after all! Perhaps I'll keep it instead for later, for ME, for the memory, to treasure, to cherish, to remember. No, this job is not easy, but who said it would be? I had the unenviable task once she had departed for the sunshine, with the sacks of clothes left behind i.e. the ultimate responsibility for my lovely, loving mum. I think, then it will be my turn and wonder who will do it for me? Well, that was another decision, another choice, for another day.

I begin with the leopard skin leggings and white studded cowboy boots. Here also are clothes, in fashion, vintage, in style, for comfort, for practicality, for occasions and then there are the ultimate favourites. I find myself reflecting, 'Who bought them? Were they presents for birthdays or Christmas, or were they bought with money given to spend ad lib, so how do you decide which to keep or throw when there are so many memories and emotions evoked when wearing them perhaps?' Then there are the 'Basics'; for example, black trousers, those worn for evenings, for best, for everyday, for casual, or sports or just plain comfort. Do you choose straight leg, flare, skinny, cropped, do you take one of each or have a spare or spares even? Then materials; do you keep stretchy ones or loose fitting, in cotton or wool? I have a headache now, it's a wearying task, maybe we should decide tomorrow, there's just too much to consider.

Where do I stop? There are still the all-important accessories to consider - coats, jackets, cardigans, scarves, belts, bags, shoes, boots, slippers, sandals, the list is endless. Of course, there's then the colour co-ordination. What if you've thrown out something really special because you have the perfect accessory? Now you need to re-visit the piles and check and sort through again.

So how can I decide what she should take to Cyprus? Maybe I need a third party. Someone who doesn't know you too well, who is not so emotionally involved, who can be detached from the emotions that are stirring within my turmoil? Mum, there really is no room for everything. You have to decide on the essentials, you have one suitcase and you are downsizing. You have a beautiful new home with two bedrooms, six wardrobes, fewer drawers and cupboards, without a conservatory, a loft, a shed or a garage. Maybe when we come to visit we could bring you a few items across that you have left behind and surprise you. Just remember how exciting it's going to be - you are going to live your dream in the sun, happy days, but to move on there are hard choices and compromises to be made. We just have to leave many things behind. Please don't judge us or me too harshly, I did what I could, but it's a heavy burden to carry, so we share it between us, and maybe in time you can forgive us for not keeping everything you wanted or needed.

And through this reflection, one begins to discern the pain and poignancy of Jackie's sense of having been left behind by her Mum too. Do you recognize any of this dilemma?

**

Another dilemma we face when we have been entrusted with organizing the end of our loved ones life is explored in this next 'letter' from my two sisters and myself to a young woman who helped us at this stage of deciding what to do with my mother's clothes...

******

To scatter or not to scatter? That is the Question!
Written in 2016

A year on from our mother's death at 90 we are faced with how to commit both her ashes and her clothes to the future in a sensitive, loving and gentle way.

Meanwhile Dad has had a bench made for the Garden of Rest in their home village. It sits at the top of the quiet village cemetery, looking down on the memorials of those who had lived and loved over many years in that Shropshire village, some with untimely dates of having died in their early years of life. The plaque on the bench reads:

Betty Bate 1924-2015 in thanksgiving for an extraordinary wife, mother, grandmother and great-grandmother

...and she was indeed an extraordinary woman.

173

Whether the ashes are to be scattered or buried has been a source of discussion and decision-making, as yet unresolved, but I find myself astonished to realise after these last few days that it is her clothes which we will celebrate as being scattered, whatever we decide to do apropos the ashes! Her clothes... I asked a friend from one of my old village parishes to come and help with this potentially heartrending task. I knew she would understand the poignancy of the task in hand as I had had the privilege of conducting her mother's funeral in the parish church a few years ago. As the three sisters we had sorted it as best we could and one of my father's fears was seeing her treasured clothes and possessions going off to nearby charity shops in black plastic sacks. Janice was a manager of a charity shop in far-off Knaresborough, a cult town, home many centuries ago to old Mother Shipton. She was an eccentric lady (if not even a witch), who had prophesied amongst other things which had come true centuries later, that one day messages would fly around the world in seconds! Thus, this market town in North Yorkshire, a watery place of history, legend, architecture and castle, enjoys many visitors, families, young people, coach trips, etc. and many shoppers!

Janice looked professionally through my Mum's colourful and stylish clothes, knowing instinctively where they would be best to go, and I am now left not feeling bereft, as I was expecting, but rejoicing. She was so appreciative of the quality of them and I saw anew as I watched how beautifully these garments had been kept and cared for over decades. "These clothes will be loved and look gorgeous on young women and pretty girls who will celebrate them as vintage clothing," she said.

We can rest now, knowing that they are in the right place, poised to jump off the rails and travel to new wardrobes, gracing new hangers ready to adorn anew young women scattered around the country: women who have chosen to invite these garments into their lives. What a tribute to our Mum's taste and style and a celebration of her lifetime's gift of craft, sewing a selection of clothing with which to adorn her own nakedness until the age of 90!

Thank you, Janice, from my sisters and myself, for helping us to be able now to move forward creatively and with new hope, through this transition moment.

The ashes themselves were finally scattered on the Malvern Hills, an evocative place of beauty, shared by my parents in their early days when they were just a couple, before being joined by the rest of the family! So, fittingly my father undertook this solemn ritual on his own, remembering the joy and fulfilment of their very long relationship over seventy years, and giving heartfelt thanks.

**

But I too must 'gird up my loins' and move on...

******

174

Continuing to Age and Reflect

A greeting card I once saw depicted a rather timid looking, apprehensive man, shoulders sagging, tired, worn, his face a picture of a heavy heart, loaded down with bulging baggage. He had stumbled upon a notice in front of a hidden doorway. *'If you see anything unusual or mysterious, just enjoy it while you can'!* I found myself irrationally so hoping that he had had the courage to choose to go through it!

Recently I chose to go through a different door, drawn by a notice: Three Score Years and Then...? H'm! This was an enticing course which I felt impelled to attend at St. Bedes Pastoral Centre in York. Ann Morisy inspired us to enter and celebrate this time of our lives, encouraged by the recent findings of research on ageing. These indicate that three lifestyle factors significantly contribute to our 'aliveness' in these years: practising cheerfulness, singing and 'doing business with God'. H'm! I have regular access to all those. That must indeed be good news for those of us who are component parts of these 'ageing congregations' which we hear so much about, usually in a depressing context! Hildegard of Bingen, a medieval Abbess, with her music, her literature and her art, indeed a woman for our time, writes; 'At birth, our Divine potential is folded up inside us like a tent. It is life's purpose to unfold that tent'.

I am writing this whilst listening to Classic FM. People are phoning in, requesting music to cheer them on their way whilst they do the 'depressing' job of taking down all the Christmas cards and decorations; finding homes for surplus Christmas presents; hoovering up pine needles, and repacking the dusty glass baubles, ready for another year. I am wondering how it is that this Twelfth Night ritual has become a time for endings and 'putting away', of sighing with relief and of 'getting back to normal'. What is 'normal?' I ask myself.

Perhaps by going back to the beginning of this book and the words of William Shakespeare, 'All the World's a Stage...' I am not sure that this is altogether true, but it makes me realise that a significant part of my life which I have not yet shared here in terms of my clothes is in that very theatrical arena. My latest such venture even finally includes Paul for the first time! The pantomime Aladdin is being performed in our local church. The producer was wise in asking me to be the genie, as I must be the one member of the congregation who has four pairs of harem trousers in my wardrobe, never mind the dressing up box! In fact I had virtually everything in my wardrobe for this part including the sari, well except for the golden turban with long purple feather, and the droopy moustache. I had most things likewise for Paul's part of Widow Twankey, except for the wig!

My earlier stage roles have included such esteemed productions and roles as The Good Fairy in another panto many years ago with wand, sparkly tiara and gown; the young maid who fell in love in Cranfield in her 'best frock'; a Brummie dairymaid in cheesecloth and mop cap; and a dastardly funeral director in a black comedy. I had the privilege of being yet another harassed maid, (this time juggling with a pile of books as usual) in Sheridan's The RIvals in the

175

studio at York Theatre Royal: and I played a wicked corrupt high priest on a York Mystery Play cart, touring the city centre, one Eastertide. The most significant part of that attire was the leather bag containing the BRIBES, discreetly hidden in the voluminous garment's folds. And complementing the time you rehearse, act and learn lines, these costumes change you and change how you are perceived in some degree for that spell. (Interesting word I automatically used – spell!) I first understood about that in my first part, the Good Fairy. Someone at the dress rehearsal said to me, 'I don't think you have any idea at all of the impact you make as the curtains open and there you are centre stage in a white very sparkly dress, floaty wings, spangly crown and wand topped with twinkling star.' She made me realise that if I was more aware of that effect, I could more convincingly 'be it' and therefore become more effective on stage. I remembered that henceforth for all my 'parts'.

But perhaps my most interesting role, referred to earlier, was as the silent 'angel in disguise' in the Brafferton mystery play locally written for the celebration of the Abolition of Slave Trading Centenary referred to earlier. It was challenging because in each scene I was playing two parts simultaneously. I was a serving wench in an 18th Century ale house in the first scene, dressed in linen cap, a woollen shawl and long messy cotton apron. Here I 'bent an ear', whilst refilling tankards, to a conversation between Thomas Clarkson and Alexander Falconbridge, potential reformers of zeal. Scene two found me 'subtly loitering' behind the Bishop of Exeter's Throne, as his eminence's chaplain, wearing my cassock of course. As a smart trouser-suited TV reporter in the third scene, I challenged Alistair Campbell, Tony Blair and George Bush about the transparency of their politics around slave labour today. In my alb, as the archangel Gabriel, I was assisting St Peter at the Pearly Gates in the final scene, when all had to be accountable for their actions in their terrestrial life! Underneath all these costumes various, however, I was also in fact the 'angel being entertained unawares', and noting the motives and ambiguous conversations, hypocrisy and self-interest of the church figures. This was an apt production for Good Friday, calling us all to account!

There are always mirrors in a theatre's stage wings, so that the last person the actor sees as he or she sets out to tread the boards is the person they are dressed up to be, and the person they have to convince others they are, just for an hour or so. The challenge is to harmonise their temporary character's inner persona with the outward appearance that their adopted clothes convey.

Well, Twelfth Night is the time we remember the Epiphany, the wise men arriving at the stable, guided by a star; a special star heralding a time of change; a sign that God is about to do something new. So I leave you with these words which I suggest resonate with the billowing-ness of the unfolding tent and they give me much hope - that if I dare to enter the mystery anew, God can still do something new in my life!

**

176

And via His 'angels', life still holds surprises...

******

Enter Stage Eight...Amazed by Joy!

 'Just turn up,' Paul and I were instructed. *In order to celebrate our 70th birthdays and Golden Wedding Anniversary the family gathered in its entirety, all generations, in our favourite holiday destination, Salcombe; some staying in our usual flat, some camping and others in the South Sands Hotel. (I say entirety, but always there are tragically two missing at any family gathering; Emma and Lorenzo. Travel limitations imposed by her serious organic health issues resulting from overzealous treatment for her leukaemia mean that we have not been together as a family for 17 years.)*

 A loud roar of excited greetings met Paul and me at the door of the flat high on the cliff overlooking the Salcombe Estuary. In the doorway laughing and joyful adults and children jostled for embrace and welcome as we stumbled in. Then, through the legs came nuzzling a small three-year-old Bertie, with shining face and smile, whereupon, with an awesome purity and accuracy of tone, pitch, sweetness and stillness, came a solo Happy Birthday song to Granny and Grandpa, followed by no hurrahs or cheers, but by an astonished silence. This song had been totally unprompted, unscheduled; he had just picked up, in hearing all the plans, that it was a birthday celebration for us; so for him, that is just what he had to do! The sound of that silence set the tone for the wonder of the whole holiday to follow.

 We knew the birthday party was to be at The Winking Prawn beachside café for one of their incomparable family barbecues. The sun shone gloriously in a blue sky. This food is of the highest quality, (absolutely NOT sausage and beefburgers, but rather steaks, king shell-on prawns, and so on) and generous portions which mean that 'one between two' is more than adequate. Three long refectory tables in the marquee, continental style, housed 20 of us comfortably. A huge dressing up basket kept the children very well occupied in wigs, hats, gowns; as a policeman, a princess, a shark, a wizard, etc, etc. whilst they were waiting. And they were waiting rather a long time as it happened, as we were of course as usual waiting for Jeremy. This time it was said that he was seeing to a prang on his car acquired whilst touring the Devonshire lanes replete with kayak on the roof. Time went by and anxious waitresses hovered, so eventually the instruction was given to proceed anyway and Jeremy would join us later: orders were taken and the forthcoming feast anticipated with relish!

 Coming to the conclusion of our meal, the excited word suddenly went round with a note of relief, 'Here he is', and looking up I saw not only Jeremy but, oh my goodness, Emma and Lorenzo; standing there on that NIGHT OF ALL NIGHTS for real in The Winking Prawn. The restaurant was silent, waitresses tearful. I of course buried my head in my hands and burst into tears. Was it a dream? Had I had one dry white wine too many? Joshua had warned them not to keep it a complete surprise in case '…Grandma has a heart attack'. The legendary owner of that esteemed establishment came over with glasses of brandy for Paul and me, offered as a gift for reviving purposes. Even all our grandchildren had kept it a secret for weeks if not months whilst this unbelievable moment was in the making. Dear Will, whose idea it was, said, 'Well, you and Dad don't value material things, and 'stuff'; you'd rather have an experience!' Kate, their cousin, told us that all of our children had 'moved Heaven and earth' to get them there, and others did too. Lorenzo's 89-year-old mother had even collected them the day before from Gatwick Airport, which has to be truly heroic in anyone's book, and taken them to her house on Dartmoor ready for Jeremy to collect on that memorable Winking Prawn evening. Emma later revealed that she had originally been assigned to jump out of a giant cake in her pink and white polka dot bikini but Jeremy wasn't able to find a big enough cake, so they had to make do with Hawaiian garlands and a big smile!

William had booked them in, along with us, to the luxurious boutique hotel on the beach, just for one night. Lorenzo joined us all on the terrace as the evening sun set and the tide softly came in, while a recovering Emma had to be in her room, quietly as ever. The hotel thought she must be a celebrity with all that was going on, including the delivery of trays of melons, gallons of bottled water and kilos of raw carrots etc. to her allergy-free room! Well, she is a celebrity in a way. I think of her as Tinkerbell lighting up everyone with whom she comes into contact, despite the suffering and constant pain and eccentric management needed to sustain her life.

I think maybe I only had about 10 minutes with her during those few hours, whilst it must have cost many hundreds of pounds, we guess, plus stress, emotion, and risk to life and limb of Emma herself and Lorenzo to bring them to the family party. Emma can only ever travel lying down with her oxygen machine, but I now have photos of her paddling with me and the grandchildren, who adore her. The next day she even headed out in the kayak onto the estuary waves!

Emma comments; I was not merely in the kayak but (with Elliot as my inspirational cox!) also in command of the oars, grasping the opportunity to revive my Oxford 'women's eight' skills in both hands and nipping round the headland to the next bay and back before retiring in the nick of time for my drip!

Emma's life style is organised in infinite detail...moment by moment. And her final scary stage would mean a middle of the night journey with Jeremy to the airport for homeward travel. Prior to that, we all returned from our supper at the campsite up the lane. It was dark as we closed and locked the flat's front door, the handle of which proceeded to come off in my hand! There we were, trapped. No way out, except to break a window or jump! Handle complete on the outside but just spinning round and round on the inside. How was Jeremy to get out at 2.00am? Another silence of wondering, and this time in addition one of complete panic! Much to the embarrassment of my family I leaned out over the rear balcony and yelled 'we are in need of help', such that ultimately we were mercifully rescued by an astonished reveller from the party below!

The holiday continued with great joy, energy and more surprises. Special for me was arriving at the pontoon in Salcombe one evening with our fish and chips to find that the children had booked the ferry for a private river trip. (I have long booked this vessel with its skipper for my ashes when the time comes!)

My grandchildren's favourite parts of the holiday experience? '...seeing Emma, and Grandma's puddings'. These included the 1970s standby, Baked Alaska, where you put ice cream in the oven surrounded by meringue and the ice cream does not melt! 'S-all-in Bread and Butter Pudding with marmalade, and Blackberry and Apple Crumble from fruit gathered on the coastal path.

On Emma's diagnosis 27 years ago, we were offered mainly words of doom about our future married and family life. But those 'potentially disturbed' siblings had now created a miracle for us all.

I am so moved and infinitely thankful for this memory without price; a generous gift of love, unity and commitment which we will treasure forever.

**

The winds of grace blow all the time. All we need to do is set our sails…

******

Aging as a Married Woman in the Third Millennium, after Seven Decades

I have spent my days stringing and unstringing my instrument – while the song I came to sing remains unsung. Rabindranath Tagore.

In my thirties and forties, in my spiritual and academic epiphany, my 'wisdom' was eventually to grow old gracefully or disgracefully, keeping my options open! After seven decades I now know the folly of the assumption that there would be a choice! I once fully expected that by maturity I would be a spiritually and socially evolved being without the pressures of raising five children and running an eight-bedroomed farmhouse and working full time; I would have learned the balance of the Benedictine life of work, rest and play (or pray?); I would have opportunity for ordered time and space; we would be economically sound, with resource for scheduled holidays with my husband; I would attend WEA classes for intellectual stimulus, pilates for bodily fitness, and retreats of solitude for the soul.

Despite having been a mother who considered that her children were self-sufficient from an early age (Hannah, I think, is exaggerating when she says, 'I was doing my own ironing at five, peering up over the edge of the ironing board'), I discover I now have what feels sometimes like a basketful of challenging puppies again, and yet I have always fully endorsed the need to be brave enough and kind enough eventually to 'kick them off the teats'.

In my thirties with oestrogen pumping round all day, and energy abounding, I was known as the Old Woman Who lived in a Shoe. Well, five were a lot weren't they? Five? A lot? Now, minus the blessed oestrogen, there are five children, all their spouses, a husband, and six grandchildren (so far!). Until recently two sets of our parents in their 90s were living three or four hours away; (so far then, twenty); none of them needing total care, of course, but entailing responsibility, consideration and assorted levels of support. A now widowed father of 94 is a concern, though a widowed mother-in-law of 91 has emigrated to North Cyprus! I realise that we are probably the first generation of ex-professional working women, who, past conventional retiring age themselves,

181

are not only still working part time but also caring for long lived parents, being on-call for grandchildren and cherishing husbands of long marriages

'But God, please oh please, much as I love, respect and admire the spiritual wisdom of Tagore, do not ask me to sing another song! I keep thinking I have sung my song, and then you ask me to sing another.' Sometimes, as I look behind me at the coffin on the trestles, in my role as celebrant or minister for the funerals I am invited professionally to lead, I think, 'Yes, I am up for the Big Sleep'. I am in no way suicidal when I say this, but tired, and aware of having lived a full and rich life. I recall a story a friend shared with me 40 years ago which I did not understand then. She said that the greatest ambition of her, busy, loving grandmother, was to lie down, put on a clean, starched pinnie, cross her hands and go off to that big sleep. Is that morbid? It doesn't feel to me like that, but a sign of gratitude somehow. Will continuing into even older age bring different issues? Do I have fears for that stage of my life? Of course I do, and also of dying. Famously, Woody Allen once said, 'I am not afraid of dying. I just don't want to be there when it happens.'

My most surprising discovery in ageing has echoed T.S Eliot; that actually life is a circle. I am getting towards the end and recognising that I am returning to the beginning and knowing it for the first time. I mentioned gratitude in ageing thus far, with much to be thankful for and greater awareness as I age that even in the dark times there is usually blessing. I have overwhelming thankfulness for my parents, my children, my sisters, my friends, and for my enduring marriage which has survived and grown through most of the major traumas which a marriage can face. I have an appreciation of continuing good health without taking that for granted. With little money at our disposal, miraculously we still seem not to be in need of anything. What is my greatest joy in life? Being able to listen to and learn from my grandchildren!

I have reflected on these pages on my life, my clothes, how they have reflected who I am inside, and on my 'calling' to serve God, and to pray. My 'calling', even in terms of sometimes a 'calling to let go', is as vibrant and real as ever it was.

**

And when I reach my end...

****

Naked and you called me

Grave Clothes, Shrouds

The shroud is the garment for which we are all inevitably destined and as a Christian I believe that there will be new wisdoms beyond this particular moment of dressing, with even having to be dressed by another. What a letting go that is. This new stage cannot be explained...it is but a mystery we enter into. As a funeral minister I offer this hope time after time of Jesus' promise for this stage of life after life... My peace I leave with you; my peace I give unto you; not as the world gives do I give you. Let not your hearts be troubled, neither let them be afraid.

'There are no pockets in shrouds'. You cannot even begin to appreciate the full impact of this phrase unless you have heard it delivered, slowly and sonorously, in the deeply indigenous, rural Yorkshire dialect. But it made me think that of course this is the one garment for which we are all destined and it must therefore be included in my reflection on clothing, with its significance in our lives.

Undisturbed Grave Clothes of Jesus.
John 20: 6-8

Peter and John, on going into the tomb, did not see Jesus' body, but the grave clothes in a certain order and the napkin for the head. We are told that this fact alone made a deep impression on John, who as a result 'saw and believed', so how was that such a 'powerful' message?

Apparently, the word 'lying' did not mean they were just remaining on the floor of the sepulchre, but rather that they were lying precisely as the body would have lain in them, in exactly the position the body had occupied. The linen clothes were empty! In verse 7 we are told that the linen napkin was neatly folded and placed by itself. Why is this significant to the miracle of the resurrection?

We look to a Hebrew tradition of the day, in order to help us understand the significance of the folded napkin. The folded napkin was of Master/Servant significance. When the servant set the dinner table for the master, he had to make sure that it was exactly the way the master wanted it. The table was furnished perfectly, and the servant would wait, just out of sight, until the master had finished eating, and the servant would not dare touch the table until the master was finished. On rising from the table, the master would wipe has fingers and mouth with his napkin and toss it on the table. The servant would then know to clear the table. For in those days the tossed napkin meant 'I am finished'. But if the master rose from the table and folded his napkin, laying it bedside his plate, the servant knew that the folded napkin meant, 'I'm not finished yet. I'm coming back'.

Jesus is coming back. Death has not been the end. Hallelujah!

From Death to Life; unbind him, let him go free!
John 11: 11-44

Here we have one of Jesus' most astonishing miracles. Nothing could have seemed more final for Mary and Martha than that their brother Lazarus was dead. Cut off from the source of life itself, having been sealed up in a tomb in that hot country for four days. Very dead. We know from earlier accounts that this little family was very precious to, and loved by, Jesus. When Lazarus was so ill, people went to Jesus with a plea for urgent help; 'The one whom you love is sick.'

But here is a strange response from Jesus. Although the cry for help was urgent, Jesus did not go immediately, but stayed where He was for a further two days, saying incomprehensibly that God would be glorified through Lazarus' sickness. And when he arrived finally in Bethany to the news that His friend had been dead for four days, He went to the home of Martha and Mary to comfort the sisters.

Martha ran out to greet Him, but Mary stayed at home. Why did she? The clue may be in Martha's rebuke of Jesus. 'If only you had been here, my brother would not have died.' Could Mary have been angry that Jesus delayed his response to her cry for help and did not arrive in time? Did she feel as we sometimes do when our prayer does not appear to have been answered? Because for most of us there are those times, are there not? 'God, where were you when I needed you?' She did not run out to greet her master and friend.

Mary stayed at home. But then these lovely words on which this whole encounter turned, Martha runs back home. 'The teacher is here and he is asking for you.' How might you have felt? You'd been feeling you had been let down by Jesus; maybe, hurt, angry, and yet here He is, asking for you.

In deep compassion, Jesus wept, and then the miracle far greater than anyone could have imagined. No, Jesus did not stop Lazarus from dying, but much more to God's glory he brought him back to life, in the fullest of senses. Lazarus will not have come back to life and then just carried on as he was before – no, he will have been changed fundamentally.

I think if I had to choose what were for me the most powerful words of all scripture, it would be these words of Jesus to Lazarus on that occasion, 'Unbind him. Let him go free'. They all thought he'd let them down, but no: He showed them that He had something far, far greater than they could ever imagine to share with them. God was indeed glorified, not because of Lazarus' sickness, but through his restoration.

The hope of the Christian gospel is that Jesus' healing can be for us today too. How? Maybe we need to be honest and perhaps ask ourselves some hard questions. How are we entombed in our lives? Are there things or people we need to forgive? Or unhealthy ways of life which we need to release in order to allow Jesus to bring us to new life? Are there ways of being we need to move on from? What is the stone we can roll away in our lives, to release us from that which entombs us; that which prevents us from new freedom, new life; from

185

being fully alive in Jesus Christ? Even to acknowledge it and to offer it in prayer can begin the process of healing. That is the hope and promise which we have been given.

When healing does occur, like Lazarus we shall not be as if those hurts had never happened. I always think it is a nonsense to say we have to completely 'let go' of these things in order for healing to have taken place. Not possible; but if we are prepared to roll away the stone, these things which were death-dealing can become life-giving. That which has hurt us cannot necessarily become 'let go', but it can become the scar tissue grafted onto our hearts; our learned wisdom, that which we then have to offer in healing to others.

What is the stone I need to roll away in my life today? Which are my grave clothes which I need to cast off? There is nothing once and for all about this. I have come to learn that we have to go on and on, not only in our own lives but in our corporate lives and, I dare to suggest, in the life of the institutional church too. I invite you to reflect on 'what is the stone which maybe needs unrolling from the entrances of our churches today?' Those dry bones coming to life is a really powerful image for God's ability to transform any situation. He shows us that he can bring those bones together again, give them new heart, new breath, new flesh, new clothing! 'I will put my spirit within you. I will take your heart of stone and give you a heart of flesh.'

I once read of a priest who says he is determined that his job will be that of a midwife, not an undertaker. When we can roll away that stone something far, far greater than we could ever have imagined may become possible in and with Him who gave all of His life for us.

'The teacher is here and He is asking for you.' 'Unbind him, let him go free.'

**

And speaking of clothes which bind...

******

The Madonna of the Cross
Luke 2: 6; John 19: 26; Luke 24: 50-51

There is a theory that Jesus' swaddling bands depicted in Nativity art prefigure the grave clothes of his death. A sculpture in the grounds of Mount Grace priory near Northallerton is a powerful testament to this theory. From the rear of this figure one merely sees a stark cross.

186

The sculptor Malcolm Brocklesby writes:

   This Madonna is not the meek and subservient figure portrayed in so many paintings, but a determined and intelligent young woman who understands the wonder and the importance of her calling as she dedicates her child to the purpose of her creator.

   She is also aware of the suffering that this will entail. The figure of the Madonna is integral with that of the cross, the stark and terrible symbol at the heart of Christianity, which is an inescapable part of her existence.

   Her expression, however, is more of serenity than anguish. She is looking beyond Calvary to the Resurrection and the way in which she holds the Christ child high suggests the subsequent Ascension rather than the immediate prospect of sacrificial death.

The statue combines the three facets of Christianity which establish the atonement (God's one–ness with his people) of Mankind – the Nativity, the Crucifixion and the Ascension.

**

187

We conclude with a reflection – Be Dressed and Ready for Service. Clothes matter! Rejoice! Enjoy!...

******

Clothing
Luke 12: 13-21,27; Colossians 3: 1-14

We have seen in this work that indeed our outward clothing expresses very much who we are inside. One of the very uncomfortable things we are required to do, when sitting in public hospital rooms, waiting for tests, operations and intrusive explorations, is to remove our own clothes, and don anonymous hospital gowns. It can feel that we remove some of our identity. We become more vulnerable and thus often more anxious. So, our clothing is a very powerful non-verbal message as to who we are, both to others, and to how we feel about ourselves.

Therefore, it should not surprise us that in both these scripture passages, a clothing image when referring to the Christian life is highly significant to both Jesus and Paul in their teaching. Jesus warns against putting our faith in money in order to secure the future. To emphasise his point that the rich man's money did him absolutely no good on the night of his death, Jesus referred back to King Solomon, the richest man in the Old Testament.

'Consider how the lilies grow. They do not labour or spin. Yet I tell you, not even Solomon in all his splendour was dressed like one of these. If that is how God clothes the grass of the field, how much more will he clothe you'...

In Colossians, the clothing image as witness to the Christian life is equally evident. Paul is speaking here to a culture which has been led astray by different cults. It would not be difficult to make a connection with today's culture of consumerism, litigation, I want it and I want it now. I know my rights, even though that might sometimes be at the expense of the rights of others. So the clothing; Paul writes in v.9, that as Christians we have consented to:

'...you have taken off your old self with its practices and have put on the new self which is being renewed in knowledge in the image of the Creator.

'Therefore, as God's chosen people, holy and dearly loved, clothe yourselves with compassion, kindness, humility... over all these virtues put on love, which binds them all together in perfect unity'.

So how can we better ensure that people see us clothed in the gospel? How can we be clearer that what people see on us from the outside reflects what is to be found on the inside of us? It is so hard not to put our faith in money to secure the future. We are very conscious indeed of that today, not only in our personal lives but in our church life too. Money matters. We need it. At no point did Jesus ever condemn the possession of it. Yet, how are we to free ourselves from bondage to it? The message and promise here is so hopeful, if we could but trust it. 'Seek his Kingdom, and these things will be given to you as well'.

188

We put on a new self in baptism, and here we are called to a mature renewal of that new self. It is not a once and for all new self. To be renewed in the image of God as today's church we need actually to renew our relationship with him, over and over again. Like any relationship we have, we need to encourage it, nurture it, grow in it, for it to be rich and fulfilling. How do we do that? Well, for a start we go to church and to other faith and prayer groups to draw alongside the God who cares for us and loves us infinitely; but there is more. We are called here to grow in knowledge and likeness to God. A lifelong journey, seeking together how to be in community so that others, just by being alongside us out there, will want to be in here too, in order to grow together in understanding of the word of God; to grow together in prayer, in discernment of listening to God's whisper in our lives.

Old clothes, after all, wear out and will become dull and shabby if not cared for! It is the responsibility of every single Christian person to be asking, how can I grow? Jesus tells us that worldly wisdom is folly in God's eyes, 'You fool, tonight your life will be demanded from you.'

What is the insurance for the work of God to continue in all his glorious creation? We do need the money to enable the work of which we are the remnant to continue, but we also need those clothes which will not wear out. The sending out of Jesus' early disciples reminds us to travel light, be generous, give away what we have and pray.

Jesus concludes; 'Be dressed and ready for service!'

******

189

Granny and Grandchildren © *Helen Ganly*

***

'Take nothing for your journey, no staff, nor bag, nor bread, nor money; and do not have two tunics.'

Luke 9: 3 (English Standard Version)